THE KEFIR
COOKBOOK

THE KEFIR COOKBOOK

AN ANCIENT HEALING SUPERFOOD FOR MODERN LIFE: RECIPES FROM MY FAMILY TABLE AND AROUND THE WORLD

JULIE SMOLYANSKY

HarperOne

An Imprint of HarperCollinsPublishers

THE KEFIR COOKBOOK. Copyright © 2018 by Julie Smolyansky. All rights reserved. Printed in the United States of America. No part of this book may be used or reproduced in any manner whatsoever without written permission except in the case of brief quotations embodied in critical articles and reviews. For information, address HarperCollins Publishers, 195 Broadway, New York, NY 10007.

HarperCollins books may be purchased for educational, business, or sales promotional use. For information, please email the Special Markets Department at SPsales@harpercollins.com.

FIRST EDITION

All photos by Jennifer Davick with the exception of the following:
Pages x, 14, and 35 by Lena Yaremenko
Pages 119, 174, 211, 299, and 305 by Lauren Volo
Page 169 by Nathanial Welch
Smolyansky family photos courtesy of Julie Smolyansky

Designed by Kris Tobiassen of Matchbook Digital

Library of Congress Cataloging-in-Publication Data is available upon request.

ISBN 978–0–06–265130–3

FOR MY FAMILY, HERE'S TO ALL OF THE MEALS
WE'VE SHARED, AND THE ONES WE HAVE YET TO ENJOY

Michael and Ludmila, Leah, Misha, Jason, and Eddie

I am incapable of conceiving infinity, and yet I do not accept finity. I want this adventure that is the context of my life to go on without end.

—SIMONE DE BEAUVOIR, *LA VIEILLESSE*

CONTENTS

With my two favorite sous-chefs, Leah and Misha.

INTRODUCTION

I was ten years old when I tasted kefir for the very first time. My parents and I had immigrated to America as refugees from the former Soviet Union nine years earlier, in 1976, when I was just a baby and they had nothing in their pockets but $116 and an American dream. They worked feverishly to build our life here; my mother, Ludmila Smolyansky, bootstrapped her way up from a hair washer at a salon to nail technician to, in less than two years, owner of Chicago's first Russian delicatessen. My father, Michael Smolyansky, was a mechanical engineer with years of operations experience, but took what was essentially a demotion to work as a draftsman at a local engineering firm. But they were free.

Still, both of my parents felt one thing was missing: Kefir. The cool, tart and tangy probiotic drink so beloved by Eastern Europeans had yet to make its way overseas. American grocery store shelves were lined with cups of sugary flavored yogurts in cloying flavors like Cherries Jubilee and Key Lime Pie, but you needed a spoon and a sweet tooth to enjoy them. Kefir was a totally different ball game. For one thing, it had billions more probiotics—living, helpful bacteria that reside within all of us, governing our immune system, our gastrointestinal health, and more—than yogurt, which explains why every European person we knew relied on it

My father at work, in the Soviet Union, inspecting a machine he designed.

1

to keep themselves healthy. It was drinkable, so no spoon was required. It wasn't sweet; the taste was pleasantly sour and slightly effervescent. Given its novel yet addictive taste and array of health properties, Michael and Ludmila knew it would be a hit in the States . . . but it was nowhere to be found.

Fast-forward nearly a decade to 1985, when my family, which now included ten-year-old me and my younger brother, Eddie, lived in a townhouse on Carol Street in the Chicago suburbs. Our basement had morphed into an edible laboratory, filled with jars and funnels, single-burner stoves and pots of bubbling fermented milk. My dad disappeared down there, spending hours a day tinkering with ingredients until the recipe was perfected. Eddie and I became official testers, and from the instant that tart, cool kefir hit my lips, it was love at first taste. In May of 1986, Lifeway Foods was incorporated; two years later, it became the first US company ever to be taken public by a Soviet immigrant.

WHAT *IS* KEFIR, ANYWAY?

First things first: You can pronounce it any way you like. Russians tend to say, "keh-FEAR" while the Americanized—but still totally appropriate pronunciation—is "KEE-ferr." Kefir is a cultured milk with the texture of a drinkable yogurt, brimming with protein, calcium, and vitamin D. But where it

---

PROBIOTIC POWER

The 12 probiotic cultures in our kefir:

Lactobacillus lactis
Lactobacillus rhamnosus
Streptococcus diacetylactis
Lactobacillus plantarum
Lactobacillus casei
Saccharomyces florentinus
Leuconostoc cremoris
Bifidobacterium longum
Bifidobacterium breve
Lactobacillus acidophilus
Bifidobacterium lactis
Lactobacillus reuteri

Probiotics live and die by their ability to survive the acidic conditions of the stomach and intestines. The *Lactobacillus* and *Bifidobacterium* are darlings of the probiotic community, especially when they are fermented in milk, as they are strong enough to survive the trek, getting to where they need to get the job done.

---

diverges from yogurt and into magical elixir territory is its probiotics. You'll often hear probiotics referred to as "friendly bacteria," and kefir is queen when it comes to these great-for-you bugs.

One cup of our kefir contains twelve strains of live and active cultures—meaning a dozen different types of living organisms were used during fermentation to convert milk into kefir—and fifteen to twenty billion beneficial probiotic CFUs (colony forming units, which is just a way of measuring a product's probiotic potential). As a means of comparison, yogurt typically contains just a handful of strains and almost no CFUs. The gap might not seem all that important, but it's the difference between a food that simply tastes good and a food that tastes good while healing you from the inside out.

The smooth, creamy kefir you see pouring from a bottle into your glass gets its start as kefir grains—not an actual grain, like wheat or rye, but white clusters of healthy bacteria and yeast that look not unlike popcorn or cauliflower florets. These grains date back two thousand years to the Caucasus Mountains of Europe, where my family's ancestors enjoyed superior health and longer lives thanks to their fermented drink of choice—many of today's residents achieve centenarian status, living past one hundred years old. This probiotic starter—also known as the Mother Culture—may date back even further: Archaeologists recently discovered probiotic remnants in the tombs of Chinese mummies buried in 1600 BCE, the remnants of fermented cheese perhaps placed there as a guarantee of sustenance in the afterlife. Homer, Marco Polo, and Genghis Khan wrote about the life-enhancing power of fermented dairy. Cleopatra bathed in it. It's no surprise; the word kefir comes from the Turkish word *keif*, which translates to "feeling good."

When the grains are added to milk, magic happens. A natural fermentation process

KEFIR'S BIRTH STORY

When my Caucasus Mountains ancestors originally discovered kefir, they considered it to be a gift from the gods and guarded the grains like priceless gems, thanks to their ability to enhance and preserve milk. My dad told me that kefir's birth was accidental; nomads who were carrying milk in sheepskin leather bags used them as pillows as they slept. One morning, they discovered that the milk had fermented. They must have liked the flavor, as well as the fact that it lasted far longer than regular milk, because they set out to repeat it. What started out as a preservation method also healed the body, and the technique of cultivating kefir became a tightly held secret, passed down from generation to generation.

Eventually, in the early 1900s, word got out and made its way to health officials in nearby Russia. Intrigued by this miracle food that could allegedly cure disease, they wished to make kefir available for all of its citizens. But first, they needed some of those precious grains. As legend has it, a beautiful Russian woman named Irina Sakharova was sent to woo Caucasus Prince Bek-Mirza Barchorov into sharing some with her. A cryptic series of events then unfolded, including a botched seduction, a kidnapping, and a near forced marriage. Ultimately, ten pounds of kefir grains were delivered to Russia's capital, and in 1908, Moscow Dairy offered the first bottles of drinkable kefir for sale.

begins and good bacteria begin to grow and multiply. The milk becomes a living food. It gets tart and fizzy. Its nutrient composition skyrockets. Milk's naturally occurring lactose gets broken down to lactic acid by bacteria, imbuing it with a pleasantly sour taste. Kefir is born.

DRINK TO YOUR HEALTH

Thanks in large part to the exploding popularity of probiotics and functional foods, and catalyzed by a global cultural shift toward food as delicious fuel *and* gentle medicine, our company has grown with a velocity my parents never dared dream of. Kefir has moved out of natural foods stores and into the mainstream markets; you can find it wherever you shop for groceries. *Cooking Light* magazine has described kefir as, "Like yogurt, only better." *Vogue* proclaimed kefir, "The health snack of your future."

One reason for kefir's surge in popularity: It's delicious food as medicine.

Kefir has grown nearly synonymous with "probiotics," and probiotics initially made a name for themselves in the arena of immune system health. Here's how it works: Even though most people think of the nose and throat when they hear the words "immune system," 70 to 80 percent of our immune system cells actually reside in the gut. Trillions of bacteria live in our large intestine . . . and

that's a good thing! Most of them are beneficial, predigesting food (and therefore making it easier for your body to absorb all of the nutrients) and keeping bad bacteria under control. They also influence certain aspects of the immune system, such as boosting the number of T cells (white blood cells that help the body fight disease) and correcting nutritional deficiencies that could leave you more prone to illness.

When you drink kefir, you're introducing millions of additional good bacteria into your GI tract, which means you're essentially crowding out the bad bugs. In addition to shoring up your inherent disease-fighting ability, the good bacteria in kefir have been shown in study after study to bring relief to individuals struggling with gastrointestinal disorders, urinary tract infections, acne, sinus infections, and more. As far as stomach woes go, kefir is a go-to choice for sufferers of Crohn's disease, colitis, IBS (irritable bowel syndrome), and lactose intolerance. Yes, people with lactose intolerance *can* drink kefir; the live, active bacteria help break down the lactose, the naturally occurring sugar in milk. One study found that kefir actually *improved* lactose digestion in lactose-intolerant individuals.

Probiotics are also now being studied for their potential impact on psychological health. Anyone who has ever felt butterflies in her stomach before a big speech or lost his appetite during a romantic breakup has experienced firsthand the link between the brain and the belly. But emerging research is suggesting that it's not just our thoughts influencing our gut; the communication works in reverse, too. With a growing body of research pointing to a potential brain-gut connection, aka "the gut-brain axis," scientists are exploring probiotics' possible antianxiety and antidepressant effects. One fascinating recent study found that when people consumed certain prebiotics (carbo-hydrates that feed probiotics, see "What's a Prebiotic?" below to learn more), they had lower stress hormone levels in their saliva compared with those not ingesting prebi-otics. Remarkably, the effect was similar to that seen among individuals taking antide-pressant or antianxiety medication. The the-ory is that by lining your gut—your "second brain"—with good bacteria, you might some-how be able to protect your actual brain.

WHAT'S A PREBIOTIC?

That's right: Probiotics need food, too! Prebiotic foods contain nondigestible components that feed and fuel the help-ful bacteria living in your GI tract. They are thought to enhance gastrointestinal health as well as potentially augment calcium absorption. Widely available prebiotic foods include onions, garlic, soybeans and other beans and legumes, bananas, asparagus, artichokes, leeks, and whole-grain foods.

Need more reasons to include kefir in your edible pharmacy?

- Consuming dairy products like kefir has been shown to help people shed pounds; the thought is that extra calcium halts cel-lular changes that ordinarily would prompt the body to store fat. But kefir's probiotic content gives it a science-backed edge over milk and cheese. We know that the intesti-nal flora of thin people differs from that of obese individuals; research suggests that this difference may be due to the fact that a high-fat, low-fiber diet favors certain, less-favorable bacteria over others. Per-haps the introduction of beneficial bacteria spurs fat loss by preventing the intestines from absorbing calories from fat.

- New research indicates that helpful gut bacteria may harness anti-inflammatory powers, potentially enabling them to slow or halt the development of certain types of cancer.

- Antibiotic medications target harmful bacteria in your body, but in the process, they also kill off your good bacteria, leav-ing you prone to unpleasant GI symptoms. If you are prescribed antibiotics to fight a bacterial infection, consuming probiotics simultaneously may help manage those symptoms.

- Probiotics may one day help prevent or ease food allergies. This is based on the popular theory that food allergies may be due, at least in part, to modern-day environmental and health changes that disturb the body's microbiota, such as overuse of antibiotics, antibacterial soap, and hand sanitizer.

- Ongoing research is investigating the potential role of probiotics in helping people with autism and ADHD. Studies indicate that many individuals with autism have significant differences in their microbiome compared with those without autism; in a recent animal study, introducing the *Lactobacillus reuteri* probiotic strain eased certain autism-like behaviors in mice with excessively low levels of this microbe in their digestive tract. GI problems are very common among those with autism, so perhaps reducing GI symptoms may somehow translate into improving autistic symptoms. A similar correlation may be true with ADHD. More research on both animals and humans is needed, but even just the notion is exciting.

- Consumption of probiotic foods has been shown to improve bad breath and ulcers; the former by replacing bad breath–causing bacteria with healthy ones, the latter via multiple mechanisms, including the inhibition of the *H. pylori* bacteria implicated in ulcers.

- The combination of probiotics for immune support, protein for muscle repair, and calcium for strong bones make kefir an ideal recovery drinks for athletes. Two-time soccer Olympic gold medalist Carli Lloyd and Brent Seabrook of my hometown's Chicago Blackhawks both refuel with it. You'll also find kefir booths at all kinds of races, from 5Ks to marathons and everything in between. Parents even love it for their kids' Little League teams, too.

In 1908, the same year that kefir became available for purchase in Russia, Élie Metchnikoff received a Nobel Prize for his pioneering work in the area of intestinal health as it relates to probiotics; specifically, he developed a theory that introducing good-for-you bacteria into your body could enhance health and even delay some of the less desirable side effects of aging. Metchnikoff's method of acquiring these bacteria involved consuming "soured milk"—milk fermented with *Lactobacillus bulgaricus* bacteria, with a little sugar added. Today, probiotics are a multibillion-dollar industry; the National Institutes of Health has launched the Human Microbiome Project, dedicated to understanding the human microbiome—the innumerable microorganisms residing within the human body—and its many roles in human health and disease. (Spoiler alert: There are a lot.) And everyone from Jessica Alba to William Shatner to Kim Kardashian is espousing the benefits of kefir. Modern science and society are finally catching up to what Metchnikoff and the people of the Caucasus Mountains knew more than a century ago; good bugs are good for you, and the road to good health is paved with fermented dairy.

MOVING BEYOND SMOOTHIES

Millions of fans drink kefir straight out of the bottle or pour it into a glass, blend it into smoothies, and use it in parfaits. And it works wonderfully in all of those forms, as well as in frozen recipes like ice cream and frozen pops. But today, more and more professional and home chefs alike have been embracing kefir for its versatility in sweet and savory recipes.

For all of these reasons, kefir is being used to enhance flavors, inject tang, boost

WHY NOT JUST SWALLOW A PILL?

Capsules, powders, and other probiotic supplements are widely available, but when you choose these products over fermented foods like kefir, yogurt, sauerkraut, kimchi, and miso, you're missing out on a slew of other vitamins, minerals, and nutrients that naturally occur in these foods. It's like swallowing a vitamin C supplement rather than eating an orange; you're depriving yourself of fiber, antioxidants, and, of course, flavor.

Dairy is known to protect probiotics as they make the arduous, acidic journey from the mouth to the GI tract, helping them survive long enough to get where they need to be. Ultimately, dairy renders probiotics more effective. And by getting your probiotics in drinkable form, you're taking advantage of the fact that the digestive process begins in the mouth, the moment you take a sip of kefir. (With supplements, your body doesn't start absorbing the probiotics until further down the digestive tract.)

Lastly, supplements may languish in a bathroom medicine cabinet for a year, allowing the probiotics to die off; dairy foods have a shorter shelf life relative to pills (although their shelf life is still far longer than uncultured milk), so you're essentially guaranteed to consume the probiotics before they expire.

creaminess, and add a dose of healthy goodness to dishes from soups and dips to marinated meats and baked desserts.

YOU CAN CREATE LUSCIOUS, BETTER-FOR-YOU SOUPS, SALAD DRESSINGS, DIPS, AND SAUCES. By adding your favorite herbs and spices to kefir, along with olive oil and some acid in the form of vinegar or citrus juice, you can create an inexpensive, homemade probiotic salad dressing. When making dips and creamy salads, whole-milk kefir can stand in for half of the mayonnaise, yogurt, or sour cream called for, allowing you to add protein, calcium, and probiotics to dishes that often fall short nutritionwise, like spinach dip and potato salad. And when you strain kefir through cheesecloth overnight, you're left with a silky smooth Greek yogurt upgrade called labneh (see page 43) that works in dips; as toppings for soups, salads, and side dishes, and much more.

THE PHONE CALL THAT CHANGED EVERYTHING FOR ME

It was late at night in 1998, and I had been working at Lifeway for about a year after college. Only my father and I were in the office. The phone rang, and I picked up. The caller was a woman from Jamaica, Queens, in New York. She had Crohn's disease, a chronic, often debilitating inflammatory disease of the intestines. Her condition had deteriorated to the point that her doctor recommended surgery to have 75 percent of her digestive tract removed. As the surgery date neared, a friend had suggested that she try drinking kefir. The recommendation struck her as absurd, she said; how could a drink from the grocery store help her when so many medications and other treatments had failed? Still, she tried it . . . and almost immediately noticed an improvement in her symptoms. As she began to drink kefir on a daily basis, she reached a point where she and her physician decided to cancel the surgery. Eventually, she stopped taking all of her medications. "I'm just calling," she told me that evening on the phone, "to tell you that your kefir saved my life."

That moment was a pivotal point for me; I shifted from thinking of Lifeway as the family business to developing a passion for making sure as many people as possible knew about the health benefits of kefir. Since then, we have received countless letters from customers thanking us for what kefir has done for their or their family's health: "Kefir kept our family healthy throughout flu season"; "Kefir is one of the only foods I could enjoy while undergoing chemo"; "My son is lactose intolerant and kefir is the only dairy product he can tolerate—thank you." Often, peoples' doctors are surprised (or, in the case of the woman from Queens, stunned). But as modern science continues to unlock the potential of probiotics, more and more health professionals are "prescribing" kefir to patients suffering from digestive disorders such as IBS, Crohn's disease, lactose intolerance and more. These stories continue to inspire me in the biggest way.

YOU CAN USE IT TO TENDERIZE AND MARINATE MEAT AND POULTRY. Kefir's mildly acidic nature and active probiotic culture help break down and tenderize protein, making it an outstanding marinade base for chicken, meat, and fish.

IT MAKES A STELLAR SUBSTITUTE FOR BUTTER-MILK, SOUR CREAM, YOGURT, OR WHOLE MILK IN BAKED GOODS. You'll notice a very understated effervescence and tartness, and the finished product will be more nutrient-dense. It also works wonders at leavening breads, cakes, and muffins. Take a classic recipe like red velvet cake, which traditionally calls for two acidic ingredients, buttermilk and vinegar, as well as baking soda. When combined, they create tiny bubbles, yielding a light, fluffy cake, kind of like those homemade volcanoes from grade school, where you combined vinegar and baking soda to create bubbling lava. Kefir accomplishes the same thing here, reacting with the baking soda to aerate the batter, causing the cake to bake up tender and moist.

(Note: Kefir's live and active probiotic cultures flourish in cold temperatures, so cooking or baking will deactivate them . . . but you won't lose the other benefits, including enhanced taste, extra protein, and calcium. Plus kefir is almost completely lactose-free, so it's a smart option for pancake-, waffle-,

or muffin-lovers whose bodies are unable to tolerate dairy.)

IT LENDS A CREAMY DECADENCE TO EGGS, OATMEAL, PANCAKES, AND OVERNIGHT OATS. Whether you're mixing just a few spoonfuls of plain kefir into your omelet batter or bathing your oats and chia seeds in kefir overnight, your finished product will have a richness that you simply can't get from milk or other liquids, plus more protein and probiotics.

IT ALLOWS YOU TO TURN CREAM INTO CULTURED BUTTER. Cultured butter is better butter, teeming with probiotics and offering a distinct, more complex flavor than mild sweet cream butter.

Kefir does all of this while simultaneously bumping up the nutrition quotient of everything it touches, adding high-quality protein, calcium, vitamin D, and probiotics.

A GLOBAL AFFAIR

The Kefir Cookbook features some of my family's most treasured recipes, like my mom's famous stuffed peppers (page 215) or her savory okroshka (page 176), similar to a chilled cucumber and potato gazpacho. I've also included recipes inspired by some of my most cherished childhood memories; my

FROM RUSSIA, WITH LOVE:
HOW MY FAMILY BROUGHT KEFIR TO AMERICA

My parents and I settled in Chicago in 1976, having escaped the USSR through a small slit in the Iron Curtain. They left to escape religious and political persecution, and to follow their entrepreneurial dreams. We were one of the first forty-eight Soviet Jewish families granted permission to relocate to Chicago. Michael and Ludmila didn't know a word of English, but they possessed an entrepreneurial drive and an appetite for the American Dream. My dad would make his way through Chicago alley dumpsters, hunting for broken electronics that he could fix up and sell; or he would buy a box of books from a church for a dollar, then unload it for $10. My mom taught herself English by watching *General Hospital* and *Dynasty* and once she had mastered a few basic phrases, she moved up from hair washer to nail technician at a salon. They worked hard and they knew how to hustle.

My mother had come to America with one true possession; a small soup pan that she used when she cooked for me—mostly homemade chicken soup as well as farina, a creamy, hot wheat cereal, with lots of butter. For her, cooking was a way to help us all feel at home. She quickly realized that the food here was quite different from the traditional Russian staples we knew and loved. Recognizing the mass exodus of Soviet Jews arriving in the US, she spotted an opportunity to start her own business, and in 1978, at age twenty-eight, she used the money she and my father had saved in their first two years in America to open Globus, Chicago's first Russian delicatessen. (Globus being my parents' interpretation of "around the world.") My mother went on to open four more delis and became an international food importer and distributor. In 1979, the same year she gave birth to my brother in Chicago's Edgewater Hospital, she became the first person to bring Nutella from Italy into the United States, with exclusive importing rights, a huge and successful business venture. Globus transformed into the top destination for all new Soviet Jews living in Chicago; customers gathered there for company, gossip, and potato pierogi.

My parents missed drinking their beloved kefir, but it simply did not exist in the US. In 1985, my parents were attending a trade show in Germany. Thirsty for a taste of his childhood, Michael stopped into a local gro-

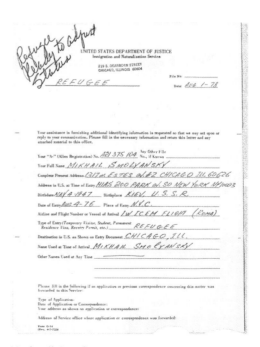

My family's refugee papers.

My mother working her JE International booth. She had many exclusive import contracts for various food products, including a vast collection of chocolate.

cery store and picked up three bottles of kefir. After a few swigs of the cold, creamy reminder of home, he turned to my mother and said, "In America, we have everything but we don't have kefir."

"Well," my mother replied, "you're an engineer—you know how to build plants and machinery. I am in the food business. You make the kefir and I will sell it." As soon as they returned home, my father obtained some kefir grains by asking relatives in Kiev to hide them in Russian children's books and send them to us in the States. Using this smuggled bit of culture, he promptly turned our basement into a test kitchen and, soon thereafter, himself into the CEO of Lifeway Foods.

Tragically, our father, Michael, passed away suddenly on June 9, 2002, just a few years after Lifeway really began to take off. Overnight, I was thrust into the position of CEO and my brother, Edward, CFO. It was one of the most devastating times of my life, but we were determined to carry on his tradition of innovation and entrepreneurship.

To my parents, kefir represented comfort, wellness, and a sense of home. Little did we know that thirty years later, we would become known as the family responsible for bringing kefir mainstream in America, where probiotics enjoy a cultlike status and everyone is eager to fortify their systems with healthy bacteria.

Piccolo Bambino Chocolate Gelato (page 294), for instance, comes from the "Little Child" nickname that Italian gelato shop owners gave me when I was a baby and my family and I spent three months exiled in Rome, waiting for the green cards that would grant us entry into the United States.

Kefir naturally lends itself to Old World Eastern European recipes. But as a seasoned traveler—I've been to Uganda, Bangladesh, Greece, Italy, Spain, Russia, Turkey, France, London, Mexico, Ireland, and more—I have so many other recipes and stories to share that come from beyond the traditional Russian dinner table. Like the grilled shrimp with avocado kefir aioli, which was inspired by the night I lost my phone and wallet in Tulum, Mexico, and found myself stranded on the beach for hours in a much-needed digital detox. Or the smoky eggplant baba ghanoush I ate at the home of a renowned Israeli chef, who allowed me to sip from the same cup that his grandfather's grandfather smuggled into the concentration camps during the Holocaust. Or Mary's Panna Cotta with Red Wine Syrup, my ode to Pearl Jam, whose concerts I've traveled the world to see forty-five times over, from the ombré red rocks of Washington's Gorge Amphitheatre to the frenetic energy of Madison Square Garden.

For me, travel is about experiencing "the other": new places, new people, new thoughts . . . and, of course, new flavors. Ever since I first tasted clear cellophane noodles on a trip to Hawaii with my parents, I've put sam-

With my family in Hawaii, 1982.

pling the local cuisine at the top of my to-do list. And whether I'm trying fiery jerk chicken at a roadside shack in Jamaica, lamb and beef kebabs in Turkey, or *crema catalana*—Spain's version of crème brûlée—in Barcelona, there's always a little voice in my head asking, "How can I re-create this dish using kefir?" It might be a traditional Russian delicacy, but it marries extremely well with a rainbow of cultural cuisines. Maybe that's because nearly every culture has its own form of a cold, fermented, and cultured dairy beverage; in Russia, it's kefir, but in India, it's *lassi*; in Turkey, *labneh*; in France and Greece, yogurt; in Iceland, *skyr*; in Sweden, *filmjölk*. I've been able to work it into hundreds of recipes in ways that go far beyond simply substituting it for yogurt. This global element will be one of this cookbook's defining characteristics, filling your table with modern dishes influenced by diverse cuisines and heritages, but all with a familiar feel.

Kefir is accessible enough for everyday use, versatile enough for reinventing family favorites, and exotic enough to offer a little decadence. Because I so love discovering and fine-tuning new dishes with my ten- and eight-year-old sous chefs, Leah and Misha, the instructions are simple and approachable, no culinary degree required. And by marrying kefir with a rainbow of beloved cuisines from around the globe, home chefs will have the chance to travel the world from the comfort of their own kitchen. Just remember to tell everyone that you made it with kefir, and wait for the *oohs* and *ahhs*.

LIVE A CULTURED LIFE

After flying under Americans' radar for hundreds of years, kefir has finally achieved avant-garde status. It's mainstream, yet still manages to maintain its cool mystery and edge. Kefir may have been a gift from the gods, but it doesn't belong to any one culture; it deserves to be shared. This deliciously curated recipe collection is designed to capture the distinctive flavor, pleasing tang, and storied history that make kefir such a wonderful, soulful ingredient, while taking you on a spin around the world, blending the exotic with the familiar for hip, modern-day comfort food.

Whether you've been drinking kefir for years, or are just beginning to baby-step into probiotics, my wish is that this cookbook will help you move ahead toward a healthier lifestyle, and that it will become a catalyst for you to play around in your kitchen and create your own recipes. I hope you fall in love with the dishes and drinks to come, that they make their way into your hearts and homes the way they have made their way into mine, and that they inspire you to bring a bit of culture into your world.

WHY HIGH-QUALITY INGREDIENTS MATTER

Throughout *The Kefir Cookbook*, you'll notice that every recipe calls for at least one organic wild or local item. Here's why:

HEALTHY, DELICIOUS FOOD STARTS WITH HEALTHY, DELICIOUS INGREDIENTS.

If you're reading this book, I know you're someone who values her or his well-being; people who make an effort to infuse their diet with cultured, probiotic-rich foods and beverages aren't generally interested in disrupting their healthy lifestyle with lots of salty convenience items, fatty processed meats, sugary colas, or junk food with unpronounceable words on the label. So already, just by picking *this book* up off the shelf, you've demonstrated your commitment to eating wholesome, good-for-you foods.

When shopping for those foods, then, it makes sense to reach for the best of the best. Many people, myself included, feel that organic and local foods simply taste better; maybe it's because I know that my spinach isn't tinged with synthetic pesticides, or that my steak came from a cow that wasn't on antibiotics and was allowed to graze in open pasture. True, the research is mixed when it comes to the possible health impacts of things like pesticides and antibiotics on human health, but knowing that I'm consuming foods that are easing—not adding to—my body's toxic load feels good, plain and simple.

Some research points to organic food as being more nutrient-dense than conventional: One new study determined that organic dairy and meat offer about 50 percent more omega-3 fatty acids than nonorganic; another found that organic produce contained 51 percent more anthocyanins, anticancer compounds responsible for giving fruits like raspberries and blueberries their jewel-toned hues. But other studies are less conclusive. Organic produce, meat, and dairy also help protect farmers' health and ease the chemical burden on the land from which our food comes. Organic or not, everyone agrees that the health benefits gained by eating a wide variety of fruits and vegetables, conventional or otherwise, far outweighs any possible health risk associated with pesticides, so if organic produce is cost-prohibitive, please do *not* skip those veggies.

When it comes to eating *local*, the science is more concrete: Locally grown produce wins out, every time. Think about the produce harvested from a local farm early on a Friday morning, destined for your favorite farmers' market not even twenty-four hours later; that seed-to-table cucumber or pepper arrives at peak freshness. Local produce also has the opportunity to ripen on the vine, accumulating more nutrients in the process. Locally grown Hawaiian oranges, for instance, contain 150 percent more vitamin C than out-of-state ones.

Fruits and veggies destined for a faraway supermarket, on the other hand, are picked before fully ripe in the hopes that they'll ripen by the time they arrive at their final destination. The instant that peach or pepper is picked, its enzymes begin breaking down, feeding on nearby nutrients. Broccoli, for example, loses half of its vitamin C when shipped internationally, compared with the locally sourced variety. When fruits and vegetables are grown far away and travel thousands of miles via plane and truck to reach your grocery store shelves, they're also exposed to more light, which further contributes to nutrient breakdown, and may be jostled, bumped, and bruised as they move from vehicle to vehicle.

Additionally, when farmers who sell to faraway supermarkets plan their crops, they tend to choose varieties by prioritizing yield and ability to withstand arduous travel—characteristics that don't always go hand-in-hand with nutritional quality.

Locavores (people who primarily consume foods grown nearby, typically within one hundred miles), then, maximize the quality of their produce, supporting nearby farmers in the process.

Now, let's talk seasonality. If you live in the Midwest and have ever eaten a grocery store tomato in the dead of winter, you know what I'm talking about: It tastes like . . . nothing. That's because it was grown on one of the coasts, picked while still green, and left to ripen in a cardboard box while being shipped across the country.

The same goes for something like cantaloupe: Californians get the benefit of super-sweet, heavy-with-juice cantaloupes, because cantaloupes love growing in hot, dry regions. But if you live in Maine and are craving cantaloupe, you're likely going to get a green, bland melon that's been shipped clear across the country from some place like Sacramento or even Central America.

Why settle? Biting into a juicy, perfectly ripe tomato is one of life's little pleasures. So if you're a Chicagoan like me, hold off on making Ludmila's Russian Salad (page 131) or my Falafel Sandwiches (page 257) until the summertime, when you can find stellar tomatoes at the local market. Similarly, save the Butternut Squash and Pumpkin Soup (page 171) and Beet and Fig Salad with Candied Pecans (page 151) for the fall or winter, when those ingredients are at their best.

SPRING TO SUMMER	FALL TO WINTER
Berries	Apples
Corn	Cauliflower
Cucumbers	Figs
Eggplant	Kale
Green beans	Pears
Melon	Plum
Peaches	Pomegranate
Tomatoes	Pumpkins
	Squash
	Sweet potatoes

UGLY FRUIT NEEDS LOVE, TOO

The typical grocery store carrot is slender and elongated, tapering down to a pointed bottom. But if you've ever planted carrots in your backyard, you know that sometimes they come out short and stubby, or maybe they sprout two legs. These not-so-cuties taste just as crunchy and sweet, but you're less likely to see them on supermarket shelves. Farmers can't easily sell ugly produce to grocery stores, so it often ends up in the garbage, making it a huge contributor to food waste. So when you see a crooked cucumber or a bumpy bell pepper, snap it up. You'll still nab all the same nutrients, plus you'll cut down on food waste by sparing it from the dumpster.

STOCKING YOUR SUPERFOOD KITCHEN

Ready to take your kitchen to the next level? Allow me to introduce you to your newest permanent pantry houseguests: the super-foods. Every item on this list is a nutrition star, delivering exceptionally high levels of vitamins, minerals, and other nutrients. Loading your pantry with these naturally nutritious items, all of which marry well with kefir in some way, shape, or form, will make it easy to assemble great-tasting, good-for-you meals and snacks. These whole, healthy foods are the difference between an ordinary kitchen and an extraordinary one.

Note: Not all of my favorite superfoods are listed here. For example, you'll notice I haven't included any refrigerated products, such as fresh produce, dairy, or eggs. I wanted to keep this list short and sweet, so we can get right to the heart of *The Kefir Cookbook*—the recipes. Besides, you don't need me to tell you that kale is a superfood.

AÇAI BERRIES These antioxidant-rich dark purple berries grow on palm trees in the South America rain forest and have a flavor best described as a cross between berries and chocolate. Unlike most berries, they boast a high omega fatty acid content that is responsible for their creamy texture. Add dried açai berries to oatmeal or muffins; stir açai powder into oatmeal or homemade applesauce; or replace the ice in your next smoothie bowl with a frozen açai pack.

AGAVE SYRUP Extracted from the same plant that gives us tequila, agave is twice as sweet as table sugar but has a lower gly-cemic index, meaning it won't spike your blood sugar levels as significantly. (Uncon-trolled blood sugar surges can pave the way to hunger and energy crashes.) Baking? You can replace every 1 cup of sugar in a recipe with ⅔ cup agave and also reduce the liquid ingredients (water, oil, milk) by ⅓ cup. Also reduce the oven temperature by 25 degrees, as agave browns faster than granulated sugar. As with all sweeteners, use it in moderation, but when you want a hit of sweet in your latte, this golden syrup is your gal.

AMARANTH This gluten-free grain is available as seeds, puffed cereal, and flour, all offering a nutty, toasted flavor along with protein, fiber, and a dose of lysine, an amino acid needed for bone and connective tissue growth that is lacking in many other grains. When cooked, the seeds have an oatmeal-like consistency and work well in polentas, fritters, and stuffed mushrooms; or mix the seeds into breads and granolas.

BEANS Nearly every respected nutrition plan in the world endorses beans as a high-protein, low-fat source of energy. In addition to providing cancer-fighting phytochemicals, beans offer an exhaustive list of nutrients and have been credited with reducing cholesterol, promoting weight loss, guarding against cancer, and more. Beans are also an extremely affordable source of meat-free protein, and they contain iron—a mineral needed for energy and oxygen transport. Add beans (kidney, black, pinto, lima, navy, or Great Northern), lentils, chickpeas, or black-eyed peas to salads, soups, chilis, and pastas; or puree into dips; or roast them

with olive oil, salt, pepper, and spices for a crunchy, popable snack.

BEE POLLEN Bee pollen is relatively high in protein and contains most of the essential amino acids, along with multiple vitamins, minerals, and even lactic acid bacteria, which comes from the bees' saliva and helps ferment the pollen. You can purchase it in grain form; the grains look like teeny pellets, and they're simply pollen that has been tightly packed together by worker bees. Bee pollen has a taste that's part sweet, part earthy. I like to add it to my smoothie bowls for a little crunch.

BROTH Use organic vegetable and chicken broth to cook up flavorful grains; to add flavor to sauces; to sauté veggies, fish, and meat; as a base for soups, stews, and crock-pot dishes. Fresh or frozen broth is ideal, but if it's unavailable, opt for boxed broth to limit exposure to bisphenol-A (BPA), a hormone-disrupting substance found in the linings of canned foods.

BUCKWHEAT Like corn in Mexico, rice in China, or grits in the South, buckwheat is a traditional staple grain in the Slavic and Baltic regions. This hardy grain can be dressed up sweet or savory, enjoyed as an entree or a side dish. Buckwheat has a bold, nutty flavor and is a complete protein source, meaning it contains all nine of the essential amino acids that your body needs to function (but cannot produce on its own). Amino acids are the building blocks of proteins, and while animal-based proteins like fish, beef, and eggs contain all of these essential amino acids, most plant-based foods do not, making buckwheat a tasty exception to the rule. (Other complete vegetarian sources include chia seeds, hemp seeds, quinoa, and soy.) Buckwheat contains higher levels of zinc (for immune functioning and wound healing) and copper (for energy) than other grains, and has developed a following among celiac sufferers and hipsters alike because it is gluten-free. Treat it like oatmeal, with butter and brown sugar; sprinkle it in bow-tie pasta; use it to stuff peppers or mushrooms; make a hearty vegan risotto; or to bump up the nutritional quotient of brownies and muffins.

CACAO Cacao beans, the dried seeds of the cacao fruit tree, are loaded with antioxidants and fiber. In fact, ounce for ounce cacao contains more brain- and cardioprotective flavanols than any other food. Depending on how they are prepared, cacao beans may eventually become cacao nibs (like a lower-sugar, lower-fat chocolate chip) or raw cacao powder. Don't mistake Dutch-processed cocoa powder for cacao powder, though; the former has been processed in a way that improves palatability but diminishes the levels of fiber and nutrients. Stir it into sauces and Mexican moles; add it to smoothies; or use it to make the richest homemade hot chocolate or mocha ever.

CHIA SEEDS One of nature's richest plant sources of omega-3 fatty acids, these small black or white superseeds taste a bit like poppy seeds when eaten raw; cooked, they swell to absorb several times their weight in liquid (similar to miniature tapioca balls) and have a mild, unassuming flavor but are incredibly filling. Two tablespoons deliver 4 grams of satiating protein and 11 grams of fiber, the equivalent of one egg white and more than a dozen dried plums, respectively. Try them in parfaits, overnight oats, chia puddings, or scattered atop a salad.

Chia seeds' capacity to thicken and swell makes them a useful substitute for eggs in many vegan baked goods. As an egg replacement, use a ratio of 1:6, chia seeds to water, to create your chia gel, then use 1 tablespoon chia gel to replace 1 large egg in your baked goods recipes.

And yes, they are the same things that grow on Chia Pets, but don't let that dissuade you. They're wonderful.

COFFEE Tea gets a ton of credit for being the healthiest beverage besides water, but coffee ranks up there, too. Regular coffee consumption has been linked with a reduced risk of heart attack, stroke, type 2 diabetes, gallstones, and Parkinson's disease. Coffee drinkers have also been found to have a wider array of healthy gut bacteria, which is considered an advantage for overall health. Adding too much sugar or flavored syrups negates these benefits, though, so drink it black or with a splash of milk.

DARK CHOCOLATE A half-ounce of dark chocolate a day keeps the doctor away. Consuming very dark chocolate (70% cacao or higher) on a regular basis can reduce heart attack or stroke risk. How? Compounds in the bittersweet treat enhance the flexibility of arteries (the opposite of stiffening, or hardening, of the arteries, a condition that often leads to heart attacks and strokes). They also prevent white blood cells from sticking to blood vessel walls, another factor known to contribute to arterial hardening. Additionally, dark chocolate is more filling than milk chocolate, so smaller amounts may help cure chocolate cravings, which can help with weight control and maintenance.

When choosing a dark chocolate, look for a minimum of 70% cacao and savor the slight bitterness; those are the antioxidants you're tasting. (I like Vosges.)

FARRO This chewy whole grain, which tastes similar to barley, has been used in Italian cooking for centuries. High in fiber and protein, it's a great addition to salads, soups, or as a hearty oatmeal substitute for breakfast.

FLAXSEEDS Ground flaxseeds can seamlessly be mixed into almost any dish, disappearing into oatmeal, smoothies, pasta sauce, and more while adding a subtle toasty, nutty flavor, along with fiber and protein. Because they're high in good-for-you fats, you can use 1 cup ground flaxseed to replace ⅓ cup oil in baked goods recipes; ½ cup ground flaxseeds for 8 tablespoons (4 ounces) butter, margarine, or shortening; or 1 tablespoon ground flaxseeds mixed with 3 tablespoons warm water for 1 egg. Personally, I like the rich flavor that butter and oil bring to baked items, but if you're vegan or your GI system is feeling sluggish, using ground flaxseeds can be helpful. Whole flaxseeds lend texture and crunch—use them in salads, smoothies, baked goods, and more.

FREEKEH Freekeh is like quinoa on steroids. Wheat kernels are harvested while still young and green, when their nutrient level is at max capacity. After roasting, the resulting crunchy kernels have a slightly smoky, earthy flavor and are high in protein, calcium, lutein (for eye health), and fiber—four times the amount in brown rice. Freekeh is a prebiotic.

GOJI BERRIES These tart, chewy gems, which look like supersized red raisins, are higher in protein than most berries. They also deliver loads of antioxidants and, ounce for ounce, contain more vitamin C than oranges, more iron than spinach, and more beta-carotene than carrots. Use them as you would raisins—in oatmeal, muffins, smoothie bowls, trail mix, or by the handful. They have a sweet-tart taste, somewhere between sour cherry and cranberry.

HEMP SEEDS These seeds of the edible part of the *Cannabis sativa* plant don't contain any THC (the psychoactive component of marijuana), but they're brimming with magnesium, a mineral with a calming effect that is known to help balance the nervous system. They're a complete protein source that contains omega-3 fatty acids, vitamin E (for healthy, glow-y skin), and can be an important iron source for vegetarians. Try them in oatmeal, smoothies, homemade energy bars and granolas, and other baked items.

NUTS Meet the ideal snack. Crammed with protein and heart-healthy fats, research suggests that just a single handful of nuts daily may be enough to lower a person's risk of death from heart disease and cancer. Different nuts have unique nutrient profiles:

Cashews have ample amounts of magnesium, iron, and zinc; almonds are especially rich in calcium and vitamin E; pecans provide niacin for energy; Brazil nuts have selenium for thyroid health; walnuts are brain food thanks to alpha-linolenic acid, a memory-enhancing fatty acid . . . you basically can't go wrong here. Enjoy a handful of nuts as a satisfying snack; you can also add them to salads, stir-fries, muffins, oatmeal, parfaits, and more.

NUT AND SEED BUTTERS All the nutritional benefits of nuts . . . in a schmear! Use them to add protein to smoothies, oatmeal, and baked goods; to impart richness to sauces, soups, dips, and dressings; in sandwiches; or by the spoonful. Almond, cashew, and sunflower seed butter get a lot of play, but I love good old-fashioned peanut butter—I carry packets of it in my purse.

OATMEAL Thanks to high amounts of fiber, magnesium, iron, phosphorus, zinc, and selenium, this filling morning staple is one of the healthiest foods you can eat. It lowers cholesterol levels and keeps you full for hours. Forgo sweetened, packaged oatmeals and stick with steel-cut or plain rolled oats, cooked in water or milk and topped with your favorite fruits or nuts. Bonus: Oats are a prebiotic.

OIL, AVOCADO Rich in heart-healthy monounsaturated fatty acids and antioxidant vitamin E, you can use avocado anywhere you'd use olive oil—in salad dressings; sautéing vegetables; drizzling over salads, pastas, and dips. It has a higher smoke point than olive oil, so feel free to try it in high-heat cooking methods such as grilling, roasting, or frying.

OIL, COCONUT Solid at room temperature, coconut oil contains a type of saturated fat called lauric acid, known to bump up high density lipoprotein (HDL, aka the "good" kind of cholesterol) levels. It adds a subtle tropical flavor to food. Try it in baked goods or when sautéing vegetables.

OIL, EXTRA VIRGIN OLIVE A cornerstone of the Mediterranean diet, extra virgin olive oil boosts HDL and reduces heart disease risk. It's ideal for sautéing or roasting vegetables or drizzling over salads, pastas, and dips.

OIL, GRAPESEED Its high smoke point makes grapeseed oil ideal for frying. Grapeseed oil may also contribute to a reduced risk of heart disease and diabetes, thanks to its higher levels of unsaturated fatty acids.

OIL, WALNUT This nutty, delicate oil contains high amounts of cardioprotective omega-3 fatty acids. It shouldn't be heated; drizzle it over salads and soups.

POPCORN Everyone's favorite movie theater snack is actually a whole grain, containing antioxidants and more fiber than many fruits and vegetables. Lightly coat ¼ cup unpopped kernels in olive oil, place them in a paper bag, rolling the edges down a few times, and microwave for 2 minutes. Enjoy naked or season with salt and pepper, cinnamon, chili powder, truffle salt, parmesan, nutritional yeast, or your favorite spice combination.

QUINOA This quick-cooking ancient grain is high in protein (it's a complete protein to boot), plus copper and phosphorus. Use it wherever you'd use rice or couscous; as a binder in meat loaf or burgers; or as a crunchy coating on baked fish or chicken.

RED WINE Thanks to the dark skins of red and purple grapes, red wine contains resveratrol and other polyphenols, powerful antioxidants credited with guarding against cancer and reducing heart disease risk. In fact, France's lower rates of heart disease—despite a national diet heavy on cheese and butter—is thought to be due in some part to their love of red wine. Resveratrol is also linked with increased life span. Women should stick to no more than one glass a day; no more than two a day for men.

RICE, BLACK contains similar amounts of nutrients to brown rice, but has more fiber and as many anthocyanins as blueberries.

RICE, BROWN has a wonderful chewy texture and is a premium source of manganese, a workhorse mineral that helps the body form connective tissue and bone and assists in metabolism, calcium absorption, and healthy brain functioning.

It also contains fiber and selenium, both of which help reduce colon cancer risk by speeding up the digestive process, thus minimizing the amount of time that possibly damaging substances are in contact with the colon. When purchasing, look for organic brown rice that has the word "heirloom" on the package to ensure you're getting authentic ancient rice and not white that has been colored brown. (White rice is essentially brown rice that has its vitamin-rich outermost layer polished away.)

RICE, WILD owes its grassy flavor to the fact that it is, technically, a grass, not a rice. It has nearly twice the protein and fiber of brown rice, plus manganese, zinc, and a host of B vitamins. One study measured the antioxidant activity of wild rice to be 30 times greater than that of white rice.

TEA Harvested from the *Camellia sinensis* plant, black, green, white, and oolong teas are all rich in polyphenols—antioxidants known to guard against inflammation. The list of diseases believed to be thwarted by tea is exhaustive; cancers of all kinds, type 2 diabetes, heart disease, high cholesterol, and more. Tea contains less caffeine than coffee, so it provides a gentle hit of stimulation without leading to jitters. If a little bitterness doesn't bother you, steep your tea bag longer than the general recommendation (30 to 60 seconds for white; 1 to 3 minutes for green; 3 to 5 for black or oolong): That astringency you taste is evidence of cancer-fighting phytonutrients seeping into the tea. Note: Only naturally caffeinated teas (black, green, white, oolong) convey the aforementioned health benefits. Naturally caffeine-free herbal teas, like chamomile, rooibos, and peppermint, taste great and may help with specific health concerns (insomnia, upset stomach, etc.) but do not come from the *Camellia sinensis* plant and do not offer the same antioxidant properties.

Matcha green tea is a powdered green tea that is mixed with water before consuming. Because you're actually ingesting the (finely ground) tea leaves themselves, you reap even more of the tea's disease-fighting benefits than you do when drinking traditionally brewed tea, in which the leaves are steeped in water, then removed. Matcha is particularly rich in theanine, a substance that has a calming effect on the brain.

WHOLE WHEAT FLOUR Because it's made from wheat grains that have not undergone heavy refining and processing, whole wheat flour nets you more fiber, vitamins, and disease-preventing phytochemicals than white flour. You can use it in baking for healthier muffins, cakes, and scones, but be aware that the dough will be a little more dense and the end product will look darker and taste a bit nuttier.

A LITTLE SUGAR

As an immigrant child growing up in the '80s and '90s, I constantly heard my family retelling stories of scarcity, all while Jane Fonda, Susan Powter, Kate Moss, and the fat-free food movement reigned supreme. Meanwhile, my parents were creating a food empire. Not surprisingly, food became a confusing, complicated, and loaded issue for me. It's taken me a long time to make peace with it, to savor a little sugar, to embrace the deliciousness that is butter, to see it as a way to fuel and heal my body, achieve my goals, and truly enjoy one of life's basic needs. That's why, throughout the book, you'll see a handful of recipes that don't exactly scream "superfood"—pumpkin beignets and chocolate gelato come to mind. And it's okay. It's all about balance; as long as the majority of your diet is filled with nutrient-dense foods like vegetables and fruits; high-quality dairy, meat, and seafood, and whole grains and legumes, there's nothing wrong with having a sweet treat every once in a while. No one can eat 100 percent clean 100 percent of the time, and in my opinion, no one should. Enjoying food—all types of food—is one of life's simplest pleasures. Let's stop demonizing ingredients like sugar, salt, and fat, cut ourselves some slack, and just eat the donut when the urge strikes.

SPICE THINGS UP

Think of your spice rack as your kitchen medicine cabinet. Besides amping up the flavor in your dishes, we now know that spices can do everything from balance blood sugar to help ward off Alzheimer's disease. In fact, emerging research suggests that humans have evolved to enjoy various spices not because they taste great, but as a direct result of their health-protective capabilities. Spices also make it easy to cook with less salt, a smart move for any health-conscious cook, but particularly important for individuals with high blood pressure.

Here are my favorites:

CHILI FLAKES AND POWDER The same substance responsible for setting your mouth ablaze—capsaicin—is also an accepted treatment for nerve pain. Capsaicin also clears up stuffy noses and may help prevent stomach ulcers by killing harmful bacteria.

TRY IT . . . on sautéed greens or in salad dressings.

CUMIN Internationally, this earthy, musky spice enjoys the same popularity as black pepper does in the United States; it's a key ingredient in chili powder, curry powder, garam masala (an Indian spice mix), *baharat* (a Middle Eastern spice blend) and much more. The oblong seeds are high in iron and are used in different cultures to aid digestion, ease stomachaches, and detoxify the body.

TRY IT . . . in chili or on roasted sweet potatoes or carrots.

GARLIC Besides adding flavor to dishes from all corners of the world, garlic contains a host of anticancer substances that, in lab studies, have shown the ability to slow or stop the growth of tumors.

TRY IT . . . in everything! Sauces, curries, soups, stir-fries; you're only limited by your imagination.

GINGER Those pickled, pink slices accompanying your spicy tuna maki? That's the same thick, knobby herb used in authentic ginger ale to calm a queasy stomach. Ginger has been used for thousands of years to treat an upset stomach; it may also help the pain and inflammation of some forms of arthritis. It has a warm, tingly, spicy-sweet flavor, with hints of lemon. A 1-inch knob of fresh ginger typically yields about 1 tablespoon of grated or minced ginger.

TRY IT . . . in Asian dishes, spice rubs, teas.

ROSEMARY This woody herb has a bracing pine-like aroma; its stems and needles actually resemble miniature pine needles. The scent of rosemary may help enhance memory and cognitive functioning.

TRY IT . . . in lamb, pork, chicken, and egg dishes; as an olive oil infuser.

SAFFRON The most expensive spice in the world is a treat for the senses, packed with a deep orange-red color, a hay-like scent, and an ability to deepen and intensify the other flavors in a dish. It has antioxidant, anticancer, and antiheart disease properties, and has been used to treat depression and premenstrual syndrome. Use it sparingly; just one pinch is enough to color and flavor multiple dishes

TRY IT . . . in risottos, paellas, aiolis.

SAGE A member of the mint family, this herb has grayish-green leaves and brings a warm, aromatic flavor. Sage has been praised for its memory enhancing potential.

TRY IT . . . on roasted pork, in stuffing, on roasted carrots.

SAIGON CINNAMON All cinnamon brings a sweet spiciness to food, but Saigon cinnamon from Vietnam tends to taste richer and stronger (imagine hints of Red Hot candy) thanks to a higher percentage of essential oil in its bark.

Cinnamon in general is credited with helping regulate blood sugar and insulin levels, and stemming the formation of blood clots.

TRY IT . . . in coffee and smoothies.

TURMERIC This peppery spice gives curry its distinct taste and deep golden yellow color. Full of antioxidants, the spice is widely used in Chinese and Ayurvedic medicine to reduce inflammation, treat liver and diges-tive conditions, and speed the healing of wounds. Turmeric's active compound, cur-cumin, is believed to protect against cancer, boost circulation, and prevent blood clotting.

TRY IT . . . in curries, vinaigrettes, scram-bled eggs, smoothies, and grated (fresh) into bone broth or tea.

CHEF'S TIP Kefir's zingy flavor pairs especially well with fresh herbs and spices.

COOKING AND EQUIPMENT STANDARDS

COOKING STANDARDS

Unless otherwise specified, I recommend keeping the following protocols in mind when preparing recipes:

BEANS When possible, I recommend cooking your own beans. Canned beans are fast and easy, yes, but with just a few extra steps, dried beans cook up creamier and chewier, plus they'll hold their shape better in pretty salads like the Kidney Bean and Veggie Salad (page 160) or the Peasant Fava Bean Barley Stew (page 183). Canned beans work best in purees or other recipes where appearance and firmness don't matter as much.

To cook 1 cup of dried beans: Wash the beans several times in a colander until the water runs clear. Soak the beans overnight in a large container with 2 cups cold water; in the morning, they should have absorbed most of the water and will have almost doubled in volume.

Drain and transfer the soaked beans to a large pot with 2 cups fresh water; bring to a soft boil, then reduce to a simmer and cook, uncovered, until the beans are very easily smashed when pressed between two fingers, 1 to 1½ hours. (Be careful not to bring the water and beans to a hard boil at any time, as it can cause beans to explode, the skins to come off, etc.) When done, drain the beans in a sieve set in a bowl, to catch the cooking liquid. (You can use it to thin out recipes like hummus or other dips.)

DAIRY Use organic plain whole-milk kefir and whole milk whenever possible. We now know that reasonable amounts of high-quality dietary fat do not harm your heart or make you gain weight; on the contrary, people who opt for full-fat dairy tend to be leaner than those who choose low-fat versions, likely because fat is very filling, so you're less likely to overdo it. As an added benefit, whole-milk dairy offers a superior taste, texture, and mouthfeel.

EGGS Use organic large brown eggs that have been brought to room temperature (about 1 hour unrefrigerated). Cold eggs don't fluff up well, leaving you with too little volume when being whipped, scrambled, or used in baking.

FISH AND SHELLFISH Use wild caught fish and shellfish whenever possible, bringing it to room temperature (about 30 minutes) before cooking to ensure it cooks evenly. You can reference *www.seafoodwatch.org* for sustainable and low-mercury fish recommendations.

GARLIC When a recipe calls for sliced or minced garlic, try to let it rest for at least 10 minutes before you begin cooking your final product. When garlic is cut, it releases compounds that elevate the levels of allicin, which is the nutrient responsible for garlic's anticancer properties. Heat disables this process, but letting prepped garlic rest allows the allicin levels to build up as much as possible, resulting in more allicin in the food that makes its way to your plate.

MEATS Use organic grass-fed beef and organic chicken whenever possible, bringing it to room temperature (about 1 hour unrefrigerated) before cooking to ensure a more even browning. Grass-fed meat contains more antioxidant vitamins and more heart-healthy omega-3 fatty acids than grain-fed meat, as well as more conjugated linoleic acid (CLA), a fatty acid that has been linked with lower rates of diabetes and cancer, as well as a lower body fat percentage. It's also smart to look for the phrase "pasture-raised" on meat and poultry labels; this means the animal was allowed to roam outside in its natural environment and was likely treated more humanely than its caged counterparts. Always be sure to cook meat, poultry, and pork thoroughly.

OIL I use organic extra virgin olive oil for everything, except when frying, when I use grapeseed oil because of its higher smoke point.

OVEN All of the recipes here are based on a conventional oven. If you use a convection oven, you'll need to reduce the temperature by 25 degrees.

PRODUCE Use organic produce whenever possible, and always wash it well before consuming. Locally grown, seasonal produce is ideal. In general, smaller fruits and vegetables are more flavor-packed and nutrient-dense than larger ones.

SALT You'll see Maldon sea salt called for liberally. This flaky sea salt is a favorite among chefs, who love its clean taste and the lack of anticaking and other additives often included in regular table salt. Because Maldon sea salt's soft crystals are pyramid-shaped, more surface area comes in contact with your tongue, meaning you can actually use less of it than table salt, while achieving even more of a flavor punch. Use Maldon sea salt unless instructed otherwise.

A pinch of salt is defined as whatever you can pick up between the tips of your thumb, index, and middle fingers. It's a fairly generous amount—don't skimp; it should take longer than a second for all of the salt to fall from your fingers.

EQUIPMENT STANDARDS

Your kitchen doesn't have to be worthy of a Williams-Sonoma photo shoot in order to create delicious, satisfying food. A handful of basic tools are all you need to gain a serious edge over the average home chef:

BLENDER Splurging on a high-powered blender will make all the difference in your smoothies, quickly pulverizing frozen fruit and ice, and seamlessly integrating multiple textures, like fresh leafy greens, thick and creamy nut butters, chia seeds, and more.

CROCKPOT / SLOW COOKER Add your ingredients in the morning, program in your cooking time, and arrive home at the end of the day to a home that smells like you've been toiling away in the kitchen all day long.

KNIVES The three most important knives to have are a great paring knife, an 8-inch chef's knife, and a serrated knife.

MANDOLINE Delivers precise, uniform cuts to vegetables.

MICROPLANE For zesting citrus and grating cheese.

RICE COOKER Not essential, but certainly time saving. I recommend avoiding rice cookers with aluminum bowls, because of aluminum's suspected link with Alzheimer's disease; go for stainless steel instead.

RUBBER SPATULA For mixing and incorporating foods, folding egg whites into batters, and scraping and removing food from bowls and pans.

SAUCEPAN For heating and melting foods and making and reducing sauces.

SAUTÉ PAN For sautéing foods, cooking eggs, searing meat, and more. Sauté pans are often confused with skillets; the former has straight sides and a larger surface area, while the latter has sides that flake up and out at an angle. They can be used interchangeably, though the straight up-and-down sides of the sauté pan make it better suited for liquids (less spillage), while the skillet's angled sides make flipping eggs, fish, and meat a bit easier.

STAINLESS STEEL MIXING BOWLS Metal bowls are easier to clean, and they won't break if accidentally dropped.

STAINLESS STEEL SLOTTED (PELTEX) SPATULA For turning fish, pancakes, and cookies; for stir-fries, and more.

12-INCH CAST-IRON SKILLET Extremely durable and, if cared for properly, naturally nonstick. Perfect for searing meats, quick stir-fries, pan-frying, etc. You don't need to spend more than $60 for a great cast-iron skillet.

WOODEN SPOONS Unlike metal spoons, wooden spoons do not transfer heat very well (so if you leave your spoon in a simmering sauce for a few minutes, it won't burn you when you pick it back up), they won't react with acidic foods like tomato sauce, and they will not scratch nonstick pans.

REFRIGERATOR STAPLES

Curate a cultured fridge with this assortment of fermented staples. Every one of these basics* is brimming with beneficial bacteria, and having even just a handful of them on hand will ensure you're getting probiotics on a daily basis. I love these staples not just for their health benefits, but for their versatility. With a generous bowl of Kefir Labneh (page 43), for instance, you'll have a base for breakfast parfaits, a mix-in for soups and dips, a cool, luscious topping for roasted veggies, a spread for sandwiches, and the start of an addictive buttercream frosting. Cultured Kefir Butter (page 35) tastes outrageous and can be personalized with sea salt, turmeric and ginger, honey and lavender, and much more.

*Except the Roasted Garlic, but it tastes like sweet, nutty heaven and is a key ingredient in my Hummus (page 154) and Eggplant Baba Ghanoush (page 156).

Homemade Kefir

It's easy to enjoy the incredible taste and health benefits of fresh kefir at home. All you need is milk and kefir cultures to create a powerful probiotic drink the whole family will enjoy. You can make kefir using your favorite milk or even nondairy milk, such as coconut, almond, or cashew milk.

1 quart milk

1 packet kefir starter culture*

In a large saucepan, warm the milk over medium heat to 175° to 180°F. Remove the pan from the heat and allow the milk to cool to 68° to 78°F. Pour the liquid into a sterilized glass or plastic container and stir in the packet of starter culture. Cover the mouth of the container with cheesecloth or a coffee filter and secure with a rubber band or string. Allow the milk to culture at room temperature (72° to 74°F) for 16 to 18 hours.

You'll know your kefir is ready when the consistency of the liquid changes—dairy kefir will thicken and may form a layer of cream; nondairy kefir can become slightly fizzy and bubbly.

Drink it immediately or cover it with a tight lid and refrigerate; it will last for up to 2 weeks in the refrigerator.

* Starter culture is tricky to find in stores, but more easily available online. You can find it at kefir.com.

DID YOU KNOW . . .

Kefir cultures can maintain their optimal bacterial concentration for up to 3 years when refrigerated or frozen!

CHEF'S TIPS

Keep your kefir away from other types of food and direct sunlight, and at a consistent temperature while culturing (72° to 74°F).

Thoroughly wash and sanitize your jars before starting a batch of kefir.

Cultured Kefir Butter

Ready for some fabulously funky flavor? This butter is tastier, tangier, and more nutritious than anything you'll find at the store. This is what butter was meant to taste like.

Sure, you can buy butter at the supermarket. But making your own takes just a little extra effort, is surprisingly easy, and actually quite rewarding. The addition of kefir yields a cultured, probiotic-rich spread. If you're able to use cream from grass-fed cows, you'll wind up with butter that's rich in CLA. You'll also notice your cultured kefir butter has a gorgeous yellow hue—that's because pasture-raised cows eat grass and flowers, which are rich in beta-carotene, an orange pigment and potent antioxidant.

MAKES ABOUT 1 CUP

1 quart heavy whipping cream (32–36% butterfat)

½ cup organic plain whole-milk kefir

In a large bowl or food processor, combine the cream and kefir. Cover it with a kitchen towel and seal using a rubber band around the lip of the bowl. Leave the bowl out on a countertop overnight or longer until the cream looks to be thickening; the texture at the top will be similar to sour cream. At this point, place the bowl in the refrigerator to chill for a few hours or overnight.

Once the mixture is cold, mix it in with a stiff whisk, or use the paddle attachment on your stand mixer on high. The mixture should turn to whipped cream fairly quickly. Keep whipping until the mixture starts to separate and the fatty part turns yellow. Once the liquids are fully separated, drain the butter in a fine-mesh strainer set over a bowl. (You can save the liquid for baking or sipping; it will taste like buttermilk and is full of live and active cultures.) Work the drained butter with your hands on a cutting board or piece of marble for a minute or two like you would when kneading bread dough; this will smooth out the butter and release any more liquid. The final product is your kefir butter; store it in a mason jar or wrap it in waxed paper and keep it on the counter in a cool place for months.

TIP These homemade artisanal compound butters make a lovely gift. Package them up in small glass canning jars or wrap them in parchment paper tied with raffia.

Sea Salt Cultured Kefir Butter

Cultured Kefir Butter (page 35)
1 tablespoon Maldon sea salt

Culture, chill, whip, and drain the butter as directed, then when kneading the butter fold in the sea salt.

HOW TO USE IT: Put this on and in everything. Seriously.

Mustard Seed Cultured Kefir Butter

Cultured Kefir Butter (page 35)
1 tablespoon whole-grain mustard
1 tablespoon Maldon sea salt

Culture, chill, whip, and drain the butter as directed, and when kneading the butter fold in the mustard and salt.

HOW TO USE IT: Spread it across a baguette, topped with chunks of Brie cheese and sliced prosciutto.

Tarragon and Lemon Zest Cultured Kefir Butter

Cultured Kefir Butter (page 35)
Grated zest of 1 lemon
1 teaspoon chopped fresh tarragon
1 tablespoon Maldon sea salt

Culture, chill, whip, and drain the butter as directed, then when kneading the butter fold in the lemon zest, tarragon, and salt.

HOW TO USE IT: Try it with grilled or roasted chicken or fish, under eggs Benedict, or on steamed cauliflower, asparagus, or broccoli.

MY FIRST TIME MAKING HOMEMADE BUTTER

When I was in third grade, Miss Tatimoto poured cream into small containers, tightly screwed on the lids and handed them out. She then played the *Footloose* theme song and we all started dancing, shaking our cream up and down, side to side, until our arms ached. After what seemed like forever (but was probably just 10 minutes), she told us to take a close look at our containers. Like magic, the cream had morphed into butter. She then unscrewed the containers and we had the chance to spread our homemade butter on slices of white bread and enjoy the fruits of our labor, just like the butter-churning, bison-hunting, covered wagon-riding characters on our beloved *Oregon Trail* school computer game. Too bad they didn't have kefir; maybe they wouldn't have all died from dysentery.

Tarragon and Lemon Zest
Cultured Kefir Butter

Turmeric and Ginger
Cultured Kefir Butter

Honey and Lavender
Cultured Kefir Butter

Mustard Seed
Cultured Kefir Butter

Roasted Garlic
Cultured Kefir Butter

Mint and Orange
Cultured Kefir Butter

Sea Salt
Cultured Kefir Butter

Roasted Garlic Cultured Kefir Butter

Cultured Kefir Butter (page 35)
1 head Roasted Garlic (page 45), pureed
1 tablespoon Maldon sea salt

Culture, chill, whip, and drain the butter as directed, then when kneading the butter fold in the roasted garlic puree and salt.

HOW TO USE IT: For homemade garlic bread, generously rub the butter into a day-old baguette that has been halved lengthwise. Sandwich it back together, wrap in foil, and bake at 375°F for 15 minutes. Or use it to sauté greens.

Turmeric and Ginger Cultured Kefir Butter

Cultured Kefir Butter (page 35)
1-inch knob fresh turmeric, grated on a Microplane
1-inch knob fresh ginger, grated on a Microplane
1 tablespoon Maldon sea salt

Culture, chill, whip, and drain the butter as directed, then when kneading the butter fold in the turmeric, ginger, and salt.

HOW TO USE IT: Stir it into tea or bone broth for an incredible healing elixir.

Honey and Lavender Cultured Kefir Butter

1 bunch fresh culinary lavender
½ cup honey
Cultured Kefir Butter (page 35)

Rough chop the lavender and place it in a saucepot with the honey. Bring the mixture to a simmer, remove from the heat, cover, and steep for 10 minutes. Strain the honey into a bowl and let cool. Culture, chill, whip, and drain the butter as directed, and when kneading the butter fold in 1 tablespoon of the lavender honey at a time until it has all been incorporated.

HOW TO USE IT: Spread it on pancakes, waffles, or French toast, or stir it into tea or coffee. It also tastes great licked straight off the spoon.

Mint and Orange Cultured Kefir Butter

Cultured Kefir Butter (page 35)
Grated zest of 1 orange
1 teaspoon roughly chopped fresh mint

Culture, chill, whip, and drain the butter as directed, and when kneading the butter fold in the orange zest and mint.

HOW TO USE IT: Slathered on scones or stirred into tea.

Kefir Ghee

Ghee is basically liquid gold. Technically, it's clarified butter, or butter that has been gently heated, causing its milk proteins to rise to the top, where they are skimmed off. The resulting oil has a nuttier flavor and richer, more golden hue than plain butter. In Indian culture, ghee is regarded as a sacred food and is used to treat all manner of ailments, from achy joints to digestion woes. It's also included in many lifecycle celebrations, from birth (ghee is often dabbed on a baby's lips before the umbilical cord is cut) to death (it may be poured over a Hindu body just prior to cremation).

A few of its advantages:

- *Ghee has a high smoke point, so it works well when sautéing and frying.*
- *Ghee does not need to be refrigerated and, stored in a cool, dry place, should last for months, even years, without spoiling.*
- *Because the milk proteins have been removed, ghee is often a safe choice for dairy-intolerant individuals.*

MAKES ½ TO ¾ CUP

Cultured Kefir Butter (page 35)

Place the butter in a saucepan. Turn a stove burner to very low, then set half of the pan over the heat, half off. (The portion of the pan with the butter should be over the heat.) As the butter simmers, white milk solids will start to migrate to the unheated side of the pan, away from the heat; skim them off with a slotted spoon. After 15 to 20 minutes, you will have your finished product.

TIP **If you've jumped on the butter coffee bandwagon, try kefir ghee in place of butter.**

Kefir Labneh

If you like Greek yogurt, you'll lust for labneh. (Pronounced "lahb-neh.") Traditional labneh is a Middle Eastern dish, the result of Greek yogurt being drained in muslin, cheesecloth, or a sieve to remove any residual liquid; the result is a creamy, velvety cheese that's so thick, you can hold a spoonful upside down and it will happily hang out, clinging to your spoon like peanut butter. Labneh is usually used as a dip (it pairs wonderfully with za'atar mix; it also loves olive oil, garlic, and mint) or as an accompaniment to dishes like chilis, soups, or tomato-y shakshuka.

Here, I'm using kefir in place of Greek yogurt. Kefir yields a labneh that's even thicker than Greek yogurt (but lighter than crème fraîche), plus it contains more probiotics. I like including it with my meze platters, but it's also great in the morning with fruit compote and crunchy pumpkin seeds or dolloped into soup.

MAKES 1 CUP

1 cup organic plain whole-milk kefir

½ teaspoon Maldon sea salt

Line a fine-mesh sieve with three layers of damp cheesecloth and set it over a large bowl. Mix the kefir and salt and pour it into the lined sieve. Allow it to drain for 24 hours in the refrigerator (or on a cool countertop). Transfer the drained labneh to a mason jar and store in the refrigerator.

CHEF'S TIP
Try substituting kefir labneh for equal amounts of sour cream or yogurt in recipes.

Labneh Bocconcini

Kefir Labneh (page 43)
Extra virgin olive oil

Once the labneh has drained for 24 hours, instead of transferring it to a mason jar, continue draining for an additional 24 hours. (Or, at the end of the first 24 hours, simply gather the labneh in the cheesecloth and squeeze out any remaining liquid.) The end product will have more of a cream cheese consistency.

Using a ½-ounce melon baller or ice cream scoop, scoop out the labneh. (You should end up with about 16 balls.) Rub your hands with a bit of olive oil and use them to roll and shape the balls. Place the balls in a container with olive oil to cover and marinate for 24 to 48 hours. Enjoy at room temperature or heat in the microwave for 15 seconds and serve hot.

Herbed Labneh Bocconcini

Labneh Bocconcini (above)
¼ cup of your favorite chopped herbs (parsley, thyme, oregano, mint, etc.)
2 cloves garlic, sliced
1 to 2 pinches chili flakes

Drain the labneh and shape the bocconcini as directed. Add the herbs, garlic, and chili flakes to the olive oil for marinating.

Nut-Crusted Labneh Bocconcini

Labneh Bocconcini (above)
1 cup of your favorite chopped nuts (pistachios, almonds, walnuts, etc.)

Drain the labneh bocconcini from the olive oil as directed, then roll them around in the chopped nuts mixture.

Roasted Garlic

Roasting garlic is an easy way to bring a touch of restaurant-quality cooking into your food. A slow roasting process mellows its bite and brings out a sweeter, caramelized flavor. Spread it on a crusty baguette like butter, try it as a sandwich condiment, or use it to season vegetables, mashed potatoes, soups, dressings, or dips.

1 head garlic
1 tablespoon extra virgin olive oil

Preheat the oven to 425°F.

Cut the top of the garlic off to expose just the tips of the cloves. Place the garlic, cut side up, on a piece of foil. Drizzle with olive oil, using your hands to massage the oil into the cut sides. Bring the ends of the foil up and together and fold over to create a tight package. Place on a pan and roast until soft and caramelized and the garlic is golden brown and easily squeezed out, 30 to 40 minutes. Squeeze the garlic out while still warm and let cool. Store it in the refrigerator in a glass container.

Basic Herbed Kefir Dressing

This make-ahead vinaigrette acts like a dairy-based chimichurri. It will keep in your refrigerator for about 1 month.

MAKES ABOUT 1 CUP

1 cup organic plain whole-milk kefir

½ cup extra virgin olive oil

Juice of 1 lemon

¼ cup chopped flat-leaf parsley

¼ cup combined chopped fresh dill and mint

½ teaspoon Maldon sea salt

Combine the kefir, olive oil, lemon juice, parsley, dill, mint, and salt. Mix and taste, adding more salt if needed. Chill for at least 1 hour to let the flavors meld (but it tastes even better when refrigerated overnight).

VARIATION Add 2 tablespoons of your favorite mustard to change this up a bit. I like stone-ground or Dijon.

Neapolitan Pizza Crust

A huge number of immigrants filtered through Italy on their way to America, and my family was no different. For most of us, this temporary resting spot offered us not only our chance at a new life, but also our first taste of pizza. Unlike the dense, hearty deep-dish pizza of our eventual hometown, Neapolitan-style pizza dough is extremely simple—just flour, yeast, water, and salt. Because it has so few ingredients, it relies on fermentation to develop its flavors and to allow that lovely, stretchy gluten to form. Here, I've replaced the yeast with my own favorite fermenter; kefir. Kefir helps the dough rise.

This recipe is inspired by a story that has been told and retold many times. It was 1979, and our family of four was living in our cramped suburban townhouse. Mom washed hair in a salon for a living; dad was an engineer. One night, as my newborn brother and I slept in our shared bedroom, my parents invited their closest friends, who had immigrated here shortly after we did, over for dinner. It was the dead of winter, freezing outside, Chicago-style. The two couples pooled the money in their combined pockets and ordered a large, $12 pizza. When the deliveryman knocked on the door, my father greeted him on our front doorstep, paid him, and took the pizza. What happened next is the stuff of legend: Somehow he lost his grasp on the box and the pizza flew high into the air, turning over and over itself as it tumbled, slow motion–style, down into the snow, landing toppings-side down.

My parents and their friends were hungry. They had no money left. So they did what any other starving, determined young adults would do: They quickly plucked the pizza and now-scattered toppings from the snow, brushed off as many ice crystals as they could, and ate.

Every time I eat pizza, I'm reminded of this story and of my humble beginnings.

SERVES 2 TO 4

2 cups plus 2 tablespoons whole wheat flour

1 teaspoon Himalayan sea salt

1 cup organic plain whole-milk kefir

1 teaspoon extra virgin olive oil

In a bowl, mix together the flour and salt. Add the kefir and olive oil, stirring until a ball of dough forms, 3 to 5 minutes. Let the dough rest for 15 minutes. Knead the dough for about 3 minutes on a smooth surface, adding a small dusting of flour to prevent it from sticking. Divide the dough into 2 balls, cover with a damp cloth, and set aside in a warm spot until they have doubled in size, 3 to 4 hours.

Kefir Farmer Cheese

If cottage cheese and ricotta cheese had a love child, this would be it. Farmer cheese is a soft, unripened cheese that has had most of its moisture pressed out. I grew up eating it by the tub; Eastern Europeans can easily go through a pound of it for breakfast. It's high in protein—3 grams in just 2 tablespoons—and low in sugar, sodium, and cholesterol. My favorite is topping it with homemade preserves for breakfast, but you can also use it to make lasagna and cheesecake, to fill blintzes and pierogis, in noodle kugel, crumbled into salads, and more.

MAKES ½ CUP

1 cup organic plain whole-milk kefir

Line a fine-mesh sieve or colander with three layers of damp cheesecloth and set it over a large bowl. Pour the kefir into the cheesecloth-lined sieve. Allow it to drain for 24 hours in the refrigerator or on a cool countertop; transfer the drained kefir to a small heatproof bowl or pot and place this in a larger pot. Set it on the stove and fill the larger pot with enough water so that it's even with the kefir in the bowl, but not high enough that the water can spill over the sides of the bowl and into the kefir. Bring to a boil over medium-high heat and boil for 5 minutes. Turn the heat off and let cool, while sitting in the water, to room temperature.

When cool, line another fine-mesh sieve or colander with three fresh layers of cheesecloth and pour the kefir into the colander, letting the liquid drain off. When the liquid has mostly drained, bring the corners of the cheesecloth

The girls chopping freshly picked peaches to make canned peach preserves that we use to make kefir smoothies all year.

together, forming a ball, and give the remaining cheese a good squeeze, holding the corners tightly. (Discard the liquid.) Use kitchen string or butcher's twine to tie the corners of the cheesecloth together and hang the kefir over a sink or bowl overnight (unrefrigerated in a cool kitchen, away from sunlight). In the morning, it will resemble densely packed cottage cheese. Transfer the cheese to a sealed container and store in the refrigerator.

STEP-SAVER Lifeway Farmer Cheese is also widely available in many grocery stores.

CHEF'S TIPS

For a cultured, of-the-moment cheese spread, fold in your favorite fruit and nuts (for a sweet, crunchy bagel topper); lemon zest, herbs, and olives (for savory.)

Canning is a fun, economical, and rewarding way to extend the life of produce beyond the fleeting summer months, and it's the perfect activity to do with your family. You can make a day trip out of picking peaches or cherries at an orchard, or just visit your local farmers' market. Now you're more than halfway there; you just need sugar, water, pectin or lemon, and some simple canning equipment, and you'll be able to enjoy that sweet fruit well into the winter. It's as close to an endless summer as you can get . . . try preserved raspberries and Michigan sour cherries with some simple Kefir Farmer Cheese (page 48), in a Labneh Parfait (page 82) or on the Waffle Orgy (page 70).

BREAKFASTS AND BAKED GOODS

Get ready to reinvent your morning meal. Kefir is a breakfast staple in our household, but it goes far beyond smoothies or a quick drink of plain kefir as we head out the door. If you've never baked with kefir, or stirred it into eggs or a frittata, or soaked oatmeal in it, or drizzled it over fruit with a little lime juice and toasted sesame oil . . . welcome to the Promised Land.

Kefir is a surprisingly versatile baking ingredient. When substituted for milk or buttermilk, its gently acidic nature yields stacks of fluffy waffles and springy pancakes with an unexpected tang. Whole-milk kefir has enough fat to lend richness to muffins, quick breads, and cakes without the necessity of adding extra oil or shortening; it also adds a shot of calcium, turning items like scones, cupcakes, biscuits, and donuts into better-for-you treats. And as somebody who loves protein-rich breakfasts—I feel like they really power me through my day—kefir is a natural choice.

Folded into an omelet or scramble, it creates creamy, luxurious eggs. Drizzled over French toast, pancakes, or waffles and topped with sliced fruit, maple syrup, and cacao nibs, it's an indulgent start to your day. And once you've followed the easy two-step process to transform kefir into velvety labneh (page 43), you can build the perfect layered parfait or elevate your English muffin sandwich with an herby spread.

The following breakfast recipes include: some grab-and-go options—Raspberry Chocolate Chip Scones (page 79) and Avocado Coconut Chia Overnight Oats (page 57) some best saved for a lazy Sunday morning—Huevos Rancheros with Kefir Crema (page 73) and Big Easy Pumpkin Beignets (page 93)—and everything in between. But don't limit yourself to breakfast. Many of these work nicely as a light but satisfying dinner, too: Magic Mushroom Frittata (page 67); Bacon, Egg, Arugula, and Kefir on an English Muffin (page 84), and Here Comes the Sun Breakfast Bowl (page 87) come to mind.

PROBIOTIC POWER

In 1988, a few years after my father began making kefir and just prior to the Moscow Summit, he sent a case to President Ronald Reagan. President Reagan thanked my dad in a letter I still have today, writing, "It's especially encouraging to know about your deep love for your adopted country and your appreciation for the great opportunities available in the United States." Shortly thereafter, President Reagan left for the Soviet Union, where he had his historic meeting with Mikhail Gorbachev, the General Secretary of the Communist Party of the Soviet Union. We were told that he brought a case of Lifeway kefir with him. I like to think that drinking kefir played a small role in bringing down the Berlin Wall. Culinary diplomacy at its best.

THE WHITE HOUSE
WASHINGTON

May 23, 1988

Dear Messrs. Smolyansky:

I want to express my thanks for your kind letter and for the cases of Kefir which I received through Max Green. Your special thoughtfulness in writing and in sharing one of your products with me, prior to the Moscow Summit, means a great deal.

It's especially encouraging to know about your deep love for your adopted country and your appreciation for the great opportunities available in the United States. As I prepare for my departure for the Soviet Union, I am truly grateful for your support and for the goodwill that prompted your gesture.

With my best wishes,

Sincerely,

Ronald Reagan

Mr. Michael Smolyansky, President
Lifeway Foods, Inc.
7326 North Ridgeway
Skokie, Illinois 60076

Chicago Scramble

The summer of 1983. I remember sitting in the backseat of my mother's dark brown Buick on our way to Chicago's meatpacking and wholesale district. We'd be stuck in bumper-to-bumper traffic on the expressway, no air-conditioning, the Bee Gees and Huey Lewis playing on the radio. Our mission: Once a week, for nearly a decade, we would drive from the suburbs to this downtown maze of warehouses and load the car with hundreds of sausages and smoked meats for Mom to then sell at her delicatessen, Globus Deli on Devon Avenue—a vibrant hub of the Russian-speaking immigrant social scene. Every time we went on a sausage run, the owner of the factory would hand me my very own sausage to snack on during the car ride home, our trunk sagging with salty, spicy, aromatic delicacies.

Today, Randolph Street is a foodie mecca, oozing with glam craft cocktail bars and stacked with Top Chef–helmed hot spots. Devon Avenue is still a melting pot of Russians, Pakistanis, Iraqis, Jews, Muslims, and more. This recipe reminds me of those downtown pilgrimages, and of my mother's can-do attitude. This dish also reminds me of my father. Sometimes on Sunday mornings, he'd make us eggs with my mom's sausages, beating them with a little plain kefir before scrambling them. The kefir made them so light and fluffy, and really coaxed out the eggs' flavor. I invite you to eat this scramble in their honor. Sausage snacking optional.

My mother behind the counter at her deli.

SERVES 4

1 tablespoon extra virgin olive oil

½ cup diced kielbasa (4 ounces)

½ cup diced hot Italian or andouille sausage (4 ounces)

½ cup diced bratwurst (4 ounces)

⅓ cup julienned white or yellow onion

⅓ cup julienned green bell pepper

6 large brown eggs

⅓ cup organic plain whole-milk kefir

Pinch of Maldon sea salt

1 tablespoon chopped fresh flat-leaf parsley

In a nonstick skillet, heat the olive oil over medium-high heat until shimmering. Add the kielbasa, breaking it up a bit with a wooden spoon. Add the Italian/andouille sausage and bratwurst, cooking until the meats are evenly browned, about 7 minutes. Add the onion and bell pepper to the pan, stir and let sit.

In a bowl, beat the eggs and kefir together until fluffy, then add the salt. Add the beaten egg mixture to the skillet and stir regularly to scramble. Add the parsley and cook until the eggs are loose but cooked through, 3 to 4 minutes.

A PERFECT PAIRING

Enjoy this with a raw salad, like the End of Summer Massaged Kale and Pomegranate Salad (page 135), the Rye Berry Salad with Herbed Kefir Dressing (page 145), or the Brussels Sprouts and Apple Salad (page 143). Emerging research suggests that eating whole eggs with raw vegetables helps boost your body's absorption of carotenoids, anti-inflammatory pigments in produce that help lower the risk of disease, especially certain cancers and eye disease.

After my mother's store closed, I started shopping for sausage in Chicago's Ukrainian Village and Polish markets. The smell of smoky kielbasa brings me right back to Mom's deli and my childhood.

Avocado Coconut Chia Overnight Oats

Craving a quick, wholesome breakfast that requires approximately zero effort in the morning? Or a grab-and-go postworkout snack that isn't a smoothie or energy bar, but still has the protein you need to rebuild and refuel your muscles? Look no further than these overnight oats. This recipe veers from the ordinary to the extraordinary with its use of kefir instead of milk; kefir's mildly acidic properties help break down the oats' tough exterior. Once you add your toppings, you'll notice a pleasant sour-and-sweet flavor combination. (Avocados bring a delicious buttery quality plus a dose of healthy fats, but their flavor is virtually undetectable.) And, since no ovens are turned on in this recipe, the probiotics really thrive.

SERVES 1

1 cup organic plain whole-milk kefir

½ cup thick rolled oats

¼ cup unsweetened shredded coconut

2 tablespoons chia seeds

1 teaspoon ground Saigon cinnamon

¼ teaspoon vanilla extract

1 medium to large avocado, pitted, peeled, and sliced

SUGGESTED TOPPINGS (2 TABLESPOONS EACH)

Fresh blueberries

Fresh raspberries

Fresh mango

Toasted sliced almonds

Sunflower seeds

Pomegranate seeds (arils)

DID YOU KNOW . . .

Chia means "strengthen" in the Mayan language. The ancient Mayans and Aztecs snacked on chia seeds for their energy-sustaining, stamina-boosting properties. Chia seeds also contain magnesium and potassium (for blood pressure regulation), so-good-for-you fats, and absorb nine times their weight in fluid, meaning you'll finish breakfast feeling satisfied for hours.

In a bowl, mix together the kefir, oats, coconut, chia seeds, cinnamon, and vanilla. Pour into a mason jar, cover, and refrigerate overnight. In the morning, remove the oats from the refrigerator and stir well. Serve topped with the sliced avocado and any of the suggested toppings.

CHEF'S TIP You'll need thick rolled oats or regular old-fashioned rolled oats for this technique. While I love the chewy texture of steel-cut oats, they're too firm for overnight recipes.

WHAT ARE OVERNIGHT OATS?

Overnight oats are simply oats that have bathed overnight in your liquid of choice—dairy milk, nut milk, or kefir. Stash them in the fridge before bed, and by the time you wake up, the oats will have soaked everything up, taking on a pleasingly soft texture. Now you have your base and are free to go wild with stir-ins and toppings, from sweet (berries and toasted coconut) to savory (tomato and basil). Think of overnight oats as a blank canvas, begging to be decorated with flavor.

Ina's Heavenly Hots

My friend Ina Pinkney is known as the Breakfast Queen of Chicago. I was a college student when I first discovered Ina's—in between classes, I babysat for a family that lived across the street from this Chicago institution and I'd stop in for her Heavenly Hots before heading over to work. Besides the light-as-air sour cream pancakes, which Ina served up with a peach-raspberry-blueberry compote, I always looked forward to her grandmotherly embrace and warm style of cooking. She was everyone's Jewish grandmother. I also loved looking through her enviable salt and pepper shaker collection; every table had its own crazy pair—Mermaid and Innertube, Toaster and Bread, Chocolate and Vanilla Ice Cream Cones.

Her third location, in Chicago's Market District (now Restaurant Row), just feet from Oprah's Harpo studio, was the spot for power breakfasts. Senator Obama, prominent national and local journalists, newscasters and politicians—you never knew who might sit down and tuck into a plate of pancakes right next to you. (Ina has even talked about running for office one day herself, saying, "One term only. I don't want to raise money; I just want to kick a little ass.")

Ina was struck with polio as an infant, and as the years wore on, post-polio syndrome took its toll. She wore a leg brace and could no longer work a full morning shift on her feet; instead, she greeted customers from a chair by the front door. Stopping by tables to say hello and make sure everyone was loving their spicy vegetable hash, baked French toast, or signature Chocolate Blobbs (a cookie-brownie hybrid) required a Herculean effort, but she never let you know she was hurting. She even starred as herself in a Quaker Oats commercial.

When Ina's closed in 2013, she gave me her Heavenly Hots recipe, along with her blessing to tinker with the ingredients to make it my own. Of course, I had wanted to try making them with kefir for as long as I could remember; it seemed like such a natural choice. Swapping in kefir for sour cream adds a satisfying heft to the pancakes while reducing the fat content; they become dense and almost creamy, with a dynamic, sourdough-y flavor profile.

> "It's better to have a small piece of something real than a big piece of something fake."
>
> —INA PINKNEY

HOTS

¼ cup cake flour (or for gluten-free, use coconut flour or gluten-free flour mix)

¼ cup potato starch

3 tablespoons sugar

½ teaspoon baking soda

½ teaspoon kosher salt

4 large brown eggs

2 cups organic plain whole-milk kefir

BERRY COMPOTE

¾ cup maple syrup or honey

3 cups mixed berries or cut-up stone fruit

Juice of ½ lemon

½ teaspoon kosher salt

2 tablespoons Cultured Kefir Butter (page 35)

FOR THE HOTS In a bowl, combine the cake flour, potato starch, sugar, baking soda, and kosher salt. Beat the eggs using a blender or by hand until the yolks and whites are thoroughly combined. Stir in the kefir. Add the flour mixture to the kefir/egg mixture and mix until smooth by hand or with a hand mixer.

Heat a skillet over medium-high heat and mist with cooking spray.

Carefully drop a large spoonful of batter in the pan until it makes a round 3 to 4 inches in diameter. Repeat with another spoonful or two, being careful not to crowd the pan. When a few bubbles appear on the top, carefully turn each round over and continue cooking until lightly browned.

FOR THE BERRY COMPOTE In a saucepan, bring the maple syrup to a simmer over medium heat. Add the berries and cook until the berries are soft, 5 to 7 minutes. Stir in the lemon juice and kosher salt. Remove from the heat and stir in the kefir butter.

TO PLATE Stack the hots on a platter and drizzle with the compote.

CHEF'S TIP Use the thinnest spatula or pancake turner that you have; Ina's Heavenly Hots have a tendency to tear because they are so delicate. Ina recommends pouring a few test ones first and eating them before anyone sees.

Winter Fruit Kefir Salad

This showstopper is a kaleidoscope of colors, a treasure chest of nutrients . . . yet not a berry to be seen. Winter fruit has its merits: Kiwi is an excellent source of vitamins C and K (the latter is needed for blood clotting), not to mention digestion-enhancing fiber. Reddish-orange persimmons contain twice the dietary fiber of apples, plus more potassium, calcium, iron, manganese, and antioxidants. Cantaloupe and honeydew both provide potassium and are super hydrating—helpful for the winter months when you might be stuck indoors amid dry, re-circulated air. Dressed in a tropical coconut kefir-and-mint vinaigrette, it's a pleasure for all of the senses.

SERVES 4

2½ cups organic coconut-flavored whole-milk kefir

1 bunch mint, ½ roughly chopped, ½ picked leaves

Juice of 2 limes

1 cup bite-size cantaloupe pieces

1 cup bite-size honeydew pieces

½ cup finely diced persimmon

Seeds (arils) of 1 medium pomegranate

2 medium kiwi, peeled and sliced

1 medium mango, pitted, peeled, and diced

¼ cup plus 2 tablespoons toasted sesame oil

Pinch of Maldon sea salt

In a bowl, mix together the kefir, chopped mint, and lime juice. Pour the kefir mixture onto a large platter with a slight lip. In the same bowl, mix all of the fruit, ¼ cup of the sesame oil, and any leftover kefir clinging to the bowl. Loosely arrange the fruit on top of the kefir mixture. Drizzle the fruit with the remaining 2 tablespoons sesame oil, sprinkle with the picked mint leaves, and sprinkle evenly with the salt.

Renegade Muffins

Between work, family, school, and all the other craziness of life, I needed a grab-and-go breakfast option that would appeal to my kids as well as me, but that wouldn't get spilled in the backseat of the car. Renegade Muffins are the answer. At first glance, I thought they looked like unassuming bakery treats. But inside is all surprise: First, the pancake batter lends a salty, tangy biscuit flavor. Then there are salty, smoky flecks of thick-cut bacon, a mild cheddar backnote, and a smattering of chives for a delicate, onion-y flavor. For the finale, a plump, perfectly cooked egg is hidden inside, at which you can't help but smile. (It also provides a boost of protein.) Make these the night before to make a busy morning a little easier.

SERVES 4

BROWNED BUTTER

2 tablespoons Cultured Kefir Butter (page 35), plus more for greasing the pans

EGGS

1 teaspoon baking soda

4 large brown eggs

MUFFINS

1½ cups dry pancake mix (I prefer the Stonewall Kitchen brand)

¾ cup organic plain whole-milk kefir

¼ cup cold water

½ cup shredded cheddar cheese

3 slices thick-cut bacon, diced and cooked

1 bunch chives, chopped

FOR THE BROWNED BUTTER In a small saucepan, heat the butter over medium heat, stirring periodically until it develops a light brown color, 4 to 5 minutes. (It will smell deliciously nutty.) Once that happens, remove the pan from the heat and immediately pour the butter into a small bowl.

FOR THE EGGS Set up a bowl of ice and water. Bring a saucepot of water to a boil. Add the baking soda to the boiling water, then gently place the eggs one by one into the water and boil eggs for 5 minutes exactly. Pull the eggs out and immediately place in the ice bath. When cool to the touch, carefully and gently peel the 5-minute eggs underwater, which will facilitate the peeling process.

FOR THE MUFFINS Preheat the oven to 425°F. Five minutes before you're ready to start baking the muffins, place an extra-large porcelain or metal muffin tin in the oven to preheat.

In a bowl, mix together the dry pancake mix, kefir, cold water, and browned butter, blending until very smooth. (There should be no lumps.) Fold in the cheddar, bacon, and chives.

Rub 4 cups of the preheated muffin tin with a little melted butter, then fill the cups halfway with batter. Set one soft-cooked egg into each cup, then fill up the rest of each cup with pancake batter to cover. Cook until the muffin tops are golden brown, 15 to 17 minutes. (A knife pierced vertically through the side of the muffin, so as to avoid the egg, should come out clean.)

This recipe was inspired by The Rebel Within muffin from the Craftsman and Wolves bakery in San Francisco.

Magic Mushroom Frittata

In most of Europe, especially the Nordic and Slavic regions, mushroom hunting is a national pastime, akin to eating pizza or playing football in America. You can find mushroom hunting maps at most Moscow and Kiev newsstands, but born-and-bred Russians and Ukrainians acquire the skill organically, like learning your native tongue. Families journey to the forest together, enjoying nature and reconnecting as they scout out and collect their delicious bounty. (And yes, they know how to distinguish the edible ones from the poisonous. I don't know how they know; they just do.)

Because I grew up in the United States, I've never had the giddy, muddy pleasure of foraging for mushrooms. But I'll tell you this: If I'm in a restaurant and there's a mushroom dish on the menu, I absolutely have to have it. My mouth waters just thinking of that rich, earthy, umami flavor. Shiitakes, porcinis, and creminis are among my favorites, topped only by truffles; their intoxicating scent and funky, garlick-y flavor make them Last Meal-worthy.

This vegetarian frittata recipe relies on protein-rich kefir farmer cheese and eggs for a hunger fix and shiitakes for their meaty texture; sautéing coaxes out their smoky, savory essence. Shiitakes are a traditional Chinese symbol of longevity, as they've been used medicinally for more than six thousand years. They're rich in B vitamins and copper (for energy), selenium (for thyroid and reproductive health), and zinc (for wound healing). And here's a fun trivia fact: Mushrooms are one of the few food sources of vitamin D, which is crucial for bone health as well as for a robust immune system. (Others include fatty fish like salmon and tuna, egg yolks, and fortified dairy—like kefir!) Just as the human body creates vitamin D when sunlight hits our skin, when the sun's rays reach the surface of these fungi, it stimulates the conversion of ergosterol, a substance found only in mushrooms, into vitamin D. Shiitakes, in particular, produce multiple types of vitamin D.

SERVES 4

SHIITAKES

1 cup plus 2 tablespoons extra virgin olive oil

1 cup sliced shiitake mushrooms

Maldon sea salt

KALE

½ cup firmly packed lacinato (Tuscan) kale, plus a few extra leaves for garnish (optional)

1 clove garlic, sliced

¼ cup sliced red onion

6 large brown eggs

¾ cup organic plain whole-milk kefir

Kefir Farmer Cheese (page 48), crumbled

1 teaspoon chopped fresh tarragon

1 teaspoon chopped fresh flat-leaf parsley

1 teaspoon chopped fresh thyme

FOR THE SHIITAKES In a medium sauté pan, heat ½ cup of the olive oil over medium-high heat until slightly shimmering. Add the shiitake slices, spreading them evenly around the pan. Now leave those mushrooms alone! Do not touch them until that sizzling sound quiets down; this will help them develop a beautiful golden brown caramelization on one side. Once that happens, give the pan a stir with a wooden spoon, loosening all the mushrooms. Cook for a few minutes more and season with a pinch of sea salt. (Do not salt until the end, as salting draws out moisture in the pan and prevents caramelization.) Remove the mushrooms from the pan and set aside in a bowl or plate to cool.

FOR THE KALE Trim the kale off of its stem and cut into thin strips. In a medium sauté pan, heat 2 tablespoons of the olive oil over medium-high heat. Add the garlic and red onion. When the garlic is slightly browned, add the kale and sauté until soft, 3 to 4 minutes. (Add a small amount of water if the kale begins to stick or turn too brown.) Season with a pinch of sea salt and set aside with the mushrooms.

FOR THE FRITTATA Preheat the oven to 325°F. Place a large shallow nonstick ovenproof dish in the oven.

In a bowl, whip the eggs with a whisk until fully beaten and slightly fluffy. Stir in the kefir, ½ cup of the olive oil, the farmer cheese, cooked mushrooms, sautéed kale, chopped herbs, and 2 pinches of salt. Pour the entire mixture into the heated ovenproof dish, and bake until slightly browned on top and a knife stuck in the center comes out clean, about 30 minutes. (If opting for the kale garnish, add the leaves after 15 minutes of cooking.)

Waffle Orgy

You've never had waffles like these before. The pleasure starts to build with thick, soft, coconut/toasted oat waffles that have a pleasing tang from the kefir, plus a little crunch from the cacao nibs. Next, you drip a warm, sticky maple syrup all over. Smother the whole thing with tart, satiny labneh and plump, juicy fresh fruit. The more toppings, the better. The finished dish will have you begging for just one more bite, I promise.

SERVES 4

WAFFLES

½ cup plus 1 tablespoon coconut oil

1½ cups old-fashioned rolled oats

2½ cups whole wheat flour

2 tablespoons baking powder

Pinch of kosher salt

½ cup cacao nibs

1½ cups organic plain whole-milk kefir

4 large brown eggs, separated

½ cup plus 2 tablespoons maple syrup

1 teaspoon vanilla extract

1 cup water

SYRUP

½ cup of your favorite preserves

FOR SERVING

Kefir Labneh (page 43)

1 cup fresh fruit (blackberries, blueberries, or sliced mangoes or bananas)

SUGGESTED TOPPINGS (2 TABLESPOONS EACH)

Toasted coconut flakes

Chopped nuts or nut butter

Granola

Bee pollen

FOR THE WAFFLES Preheat your waffle maker.

In a saucepan, melt ¼ cup of the coconut oil over medium heat. Add the oats and toast them, stirring periodically, until they develop a light brown color, 5 to 7 minutes. Once that happens, remove the pan from the heat and immediately pour the oats into a bowl. Set the bowl aside to cool.

In a separate bowl, stir together the flour, baking powder, salt, and cacao nibs.

In a third bowl, whisk together the kefir, egg yolks, 2 tablespoons of the maple syrup, ¼ cup of the coconut oil (melted), the vanilla, and water. Add the dry ingredients to the wet ingredients, stirring until well incorporated.

In a fourth bowl, with an electric mixer, beat the egg whites until stiff peaks form. Fold half of the beaten egg whites into the batter, then fold in the second half.

Melt the remaining 1 tablespoon coconut oil and use it to brush both sides of the preheated waffle maker. Add enough batter to coat about two-thirds of the bottom of the waffle maker (when you close it, the top will press down, spreading the batter out). Cook the waffles according to the manufacturer's instructions. Repeat for the remaining waffles.

FOR THE SYRUP In a saucepan, heat the remaining ½ cup maple syrup and the preserves over medium heat until they melt and form a syrup, 3 to 5 minutes.

TO PLATE This dish is best enjoyed as a group. Stack the waffles on a plate, drizzle with the syrup, dollop liberally with the labneh, sprinkle with the fresh fruit and any toppings. Surrender.

CHEF'S TIP It takes care to properly fold beaten egg whites into a recipe; you want to go slowly to preserve their wonderful airiness. Place half of the beaten whites on top of the batter, then use a large rubber spatula to bisect the whites down the middle. Next, scoop and fold one half over the other and into the batter. Turn the bowl 90 degrees and slowly repeat, continuing until the batter is fully incorporated. This technique is also helpful when making mousses, soufflés, and angel food cake.

Huevos Rancheros with Kefir Crema

There's so much to love about Mexican food: Fall-apart pork carnitas; tamales stuffed with queso and bundled in plantain husks; street elote doused with spicy mayonnaise, lime, and Cotija cheese; deep, chocolaty moles. But none are as easy and accessible as huevos rancheros—a sunny-side up egg lounging in a pool of spicy tomato salsa, served atop lightly fried tortillas. Named after badass Mexican ranchers who used to devour salsa-topped eggs during their midmorning break, it's a hearty, traditional way to start your day. Traditional huevos rancheros is served with sour cream; here, I mix kefir with cilantro and red onions into a cool crema for drizzling over the final dish.

SERVES 4

KEFIR CREMA

½ cup organic plain whole-milk kefir

¾ cup loosely packed chopped cilantro

½ cup diced red onion

Maldon sea salt

PICO DE GALLO

3 medium tomatoes, chopped

Juice of ½ lime

HUEVOS RANCHEROS

1 cup refried beans

3 tablespoons extra virgin olive oil

4 corn tortillas

4 large brown eggs

FOR SERVING

1 avocado, pitted, peeled, and sliced

½ cup shredded Monterey Jack cheese

FOR THE KEFIR CREMA In a bowl, mix together the kefir, ¼ cup each of the cilantro and red onion, and a pinch of sea salt. Set aside.

FOR THE PICO DE GALLO In a bowl, combine the chopped tomatoes, lime juice, a pinch of salt, and the remaining ¼ cup red onion and ½ cup cilantro. Set aside.

FOR THE HUEVOS RANCHEROS In a saucepan, reheat the beans over low heat, stirring until heated through.

Meanwhile, in a large frying pan, heat 2 tablespoons of the olive oil over medium heat. Add 1 tortilla at a time, heating until each tortilla is lightly crispy around the edges but still soft in the center, about 15 seconds per side. Transfer the tortillas to a plate.

To that same pan, add the remaining 1 tablespoon oil, turning the pan to coat the bottom. Once the oil is slightly shimmering, crack the eggs directly into the pan. Cover the pan with a lid and cook until the whites are set on top but the yolks are still runny, 5 to 6 minutes. Sprinkle with a pinch of sea salt.

TO PLATE Place 1 tortilla on each of four dishes. Spread a thin layer of cooked beans (about 2 tablespoons) on each tortilla, then slip an egg of top, followed by a few avocado slices, a little shredded Monterey Jack, and a tablespoon of pico de gallo. Drizzle a spoonful of the kefir *crema* over the top and serve.

STEP-SAVER Use 4 tablespoons of your favorite salsa in place of the pico de gallo.

CHEF'S TIP When plating, try to leave the yolks exposed—it's just prettier that way.

Kasha and Kefir Breakfast Bowl

This breakfast bowl was inspired by a favorite childhood breakfast of mine: гречневая каша (grechnevaya kasha). My mom would cook up a batch of kasha, ladle some into a bowl for me along with warm milk, a generous pat of butter, and a sprinkle of sugar. Eating it felt like being wrapped up in a cozy blanket.

SERVES 4

KASHA

1 large brown egg

1 cup medium-cut cracked buckwheat

1 tablespoon Cultured Kefir Butter (page 35)

2 cups water

Pinch Maldon sea salt

KEFIR

1 cup organic plain whole-milk kefir

1 cup raspberries

1 tablespoon honey

SUGGESTED TOPPINGS (2 TABLESPOONS OF EACH)

Toasted coconut flakes

Chopped walnuts

Shredded carrots

Dried chopped persimmons

Tangerine segments

Cacao nibs

DID YOU KNOW . . .

If you've ever slurped ramen made with soba noodles, you've eaten buckwheat! Soba is the Japanese word for buckwheat.

FOR THE KASHA Use a fork to beat the egg until fluffy. Pour the kasha into a bowl and add the egg, coating the buckwheat evenly. In a small saucepan, melt the kefir butter over medium heat. Add the buckwheat/egg mixture, toasting it until a nutty smell is achieved, 2 to 3 minutes. Add the water and salt and bring to a simmer, then cover and simmer over low heat until the buckwheat is soft and fluffy, about 10 minutes. Remove from the heat, uncover, and let it sit, untouched, for 15 minutes.

FOR THE KEFIR In a blender, blend the kefir, raspberries, and honey together to make a sauce.

TO PLATE Divide the kasha among four bowls. Top with the kefir sauce and any of your favorite toppings.

CHEF'S TIP Try prepping a big batch of buckwheat on a Sunday night and dip into it all week long. Treat it like oatmeal one morning (bananas, slivered almonds, and a plain kefir drizzle is a tasty combination), as lunch (in a grain bowl), or a dinner side dish (with sautéed garlic and fried onions) the next.

Raspberry Chocolate Chip Scones

Meet my version of an energy bar. About 30 minutes before a workout, I'll grab one of these scones, plus some coffee and a gulp of kefir; the whole wheat flour gives me the sustained energy I need to make it through a five-mile run or an hour-long SoulCycle class . . . or just a normal, hectic day.

If you fear carbs, you're probably turning the page right now. Don't. I used to be scared of carbs, too; but now, I embrace them. We need sugars, starches, and fiber for almost every bodily process, from energy and physical movement to learning and memory. Of course, quality matters—the healthiest carbohydrates are the least processed ones, like whole grains, fruits, vegetables, and beans. Classic scone recipes rely on all-purpose white flour—flour made from wheat that has been processed and refined. Unfortunately, much of the nutrition is lost in the refining process. This recipe uses whole wheat flour, meaning far fewer vitamins, minerals, antioxidants, and fiber are lost during processing. And unlike white flour, which the body quickly absorbs, causing your blood sugar to spike and then crash, whole wheat flour stays with and sustains you.

The raspberries deliver a pretty blush-tinged hue, just like your cheeks after a good workout (their vitamin C also helps your body absorb the iron from the whole wheat flour), and a little sour tang to this doughy treat. Dark chocolate chips offer a hit of sweetness; kids adore this recipe. If you're not exercising but instead are lazing around on a weekend morning, try them with some Cultured Kefir Butter (page 35) and a sprinkle of sea salt. Either way, I guarantee you'll get your glow on.

SERVES 4

1 stick (4 ounces) cold unsalted butter

2 cups whole wheat flour

¼ teaspoon baking soda

¼ teaspoon baking powder

½ teaspoon Maldon sea salt

⅓ cup firmly packed dark brown sugar, or ½ cup coconut sugar

½ cup dark chocolate chips

1 cup organic plain whole-milk kefir

½ pint raspberries

Preheat the oven to 425°F. Line a baking sheet with parchment paper.

Dice the butter into pea-size pieces and chill for 5 minutes. Meanwhile, sift together the flour, baking soda, baking powder, sea salt, and sugar.

Add the chilled butter to the dry ingredients and loosely incorporate with a wooden spoon. Add the chocolate chips to the mixture, followed by the kefir, mixing gently until loosely incorporated. (The dough should be "shaggy" looking.) Add the raspberries and as you incorporate them into the dough, crush them gently with your spoon. Chill the mixture in the refrigerator for 10 minutes to set.

Scoop out 2 heaping tablespoons of the mixture and use your hands to loosely form a small disk or triangular scone shape. Place on the lined baking sheet. Bake for 12 minutes and let rest for an additional 10 minutes before enjoying.

NOTE These scones can also be served as a dessert: Warm them up (5 minutes in a 375°F oven) and top with Piccolo Bambino Chocolate Gelato (page 294).

Build Your Own Labneh Parfait

Parfaits are like small-scale works of art, and so easy to assemble. Just start with a batch of rich, creamy Kefir Labneh (page 43), then grab a parfait glass and begin layering ½ cup of the labneh with a variety of crunchy and chewy toppings. (If you don't have any labneh, regular whole-milk kefir works too; the layers just won't be as distinct.) You'll be starting your day off with protein and a dose of fermented goodness, plus most of the crunchy toppings in Column A are prebiotics, making them the perfect probiotic parfait partner.

Try this simple formula:

COLUMN A (CRUNCHY)

CHOOSE NO MORE THAN 2

Roasted chopped nuts: almonds, walnuts, pecans, cashews, peanuts

Toasted seeds: sesame, hemp, sunflower

Cacao nibs

Granola

Slow-roasted olives (savory)

COLUMN B (CHEWY)

CHOOSE NO MORE THAN 2

Dried fruit: goji berries, cranberries, cherries, blueberries

Unsweetened coconut flakes

Preserved lemon (savory and sweet)

Sun-dried tomatoes (savory)

MUST-TRY COMBINATIONS

Walnuts + dried goji berries + fresh mandarin segments + honey

Sunflower seeds + preserved lemon + diced apricots + olive oil + mint

Cacao nibs+ coconut flakes + pomegranate seeds (arils) + orange juice

Pumpkin seeds + dried cherries + diced fresh peaches + sumac

COLUMN C (FRESH FRUIT)

CHOOSE NO MORE THAN 2

Berries: blueberries, raspberries, blackberries, strawberries

Diced stone fruit: apricot, plums, peaches

Pomegranate seeds (arils)

Diced tree fruits: apples, pears, Asian pears

Citrus: kumquats, mandarin segments, orange segments

COLUMN D

A DRIZZLE OR A DASH OF 1

Honey

Maldon sea salt

Extra virgin olive oil

Citrus juice

Spices: sumac, smoked paprika, Aleppo pepper, za'atar, cumin, coriander

Fresh herbs: mint, basil, cilantro, flat-leaf parsley

Bacon, Egg, Arugula, and Kefir on an English Muffin

I used to sing "Do You Know the Muffin Man?" to our girls when they were little, never realizing that the Muffin Man's delicious wares were, in fact, English muffins. During a recent trip to England, though, I learned that Drury Lane is located in London, and I had the opportunity to taste a genuine crumpet (aka English muffin). You bite through the cornmeal-dusted exterior to find an inside that's fluffy and chewy, and their craggy texture practically begs to be flooded with butter, jam, or whatever topping you like. What's not to love about these nooked and crannied little treats? Here, I've stacked them with bacon, egg, peppery arugula, and a schmear of kefir labneh for a modern, foodie take on an egg sandwich.

SERVES 4

EGGS
4 teaspoons extra virgin olive oil

4 large brown eggs

Maldon sea salt and freshly cracked black pepper

MUFFINS
4 whole wheat English muffins, split

3/4 cup Kefir Labneh (page 43)

2 tablespoons chopped chives

6 slices thick-cut organic bacon, cooked and halved

1 cup firmly packed wild arugula

FOR THE EGGS Start with a pot large enough to hold four 4-inch-wide porcelain ramekins. Place the pot on the stove and fill it with 1 inch of hot water and bring to a simmer. Meanwhile, coat the insides of each of four shallow 4-inch-wide ramekins with 1 teaspoon olive oil. Crack one egg into each ramekin, sprinkle with sea salt and black pepper to taste. Place the ramekins into the pot of simmering water, cover, and cook for 6 minutes. Remove the ramekins with tongs. Set aside.

FOR THE MUFFINS Toast the English muffins to a light brown. In a small bowl, stir together the labneh and chives. Place 2 muffin halves on each plate and spread each half with the labneh. Place a poached egg on the bottom half of each muffin and top with 3 pieces of bacon and ¼ cup packed arugula. Cap each one off with the English muffin top.

DID YOU KNOW . . .

The days of tossing out the yolks are over. Health and nutrition experts now know that eating egg yolks, which happen to contain a hefty amount of cholesterol, won't actually raise the cholesterol levels in your blood. What they *will* do: Provide you with iron, folate, a nutrient called choline (especially important for pregnant women), and lutein and zeaxanthin for eye health. That's one reason you'll notice that not a single recipe in this book calls for egg whites only. (The other reason: Egg yolks taste *good*.)

Besides, everything tastes better with an egg on it. So dig in, yolks and all.

Here Comes the Sun Breakfast Bowl

When my father was a young man living in the USSR in the '60s, he was able to get his hands on a few black market Beatles and Led Zeppelin albums. Don't ask me how; he just did. He was in his twenties, curious about America and anxiously hopeful for the chance to one day live there. At home, he would quietly play his vinyl records, dreaming of a different existence, aware that simply listening to these censored albums put him at risk of being arrested. His mechanical engineering background also enabled him to fix up an old radio he found in an alley and use it to pick up Voice of America, a US-based broadcast that the Soviet Union purposefully jammed. This, too, could land him in jail, or worse, but he risked it all, hungry for news and information further confirming what he felt in his heart . . . escaping the Soviet Union was the only option.

My father embraced all this country had to offer. He dearly believed in its values—values not offered in his homeland, such as freedom of speech, freedom of the press, civil liberties, capitalism, and the possibility of achieving the American Dream. He became an expert in explaining the ways of American life and offering support and advice to anyone who asked. To this day, complete strangers still thank me with tears in their eyes for the help my father offered them in a strange foreign land. I can imagine him singing along to his Abbey Road album, now safely on the right side of the Iron Curtain.

My father listening to his black market records.

HERE COMES THE SUN BREAKFAST BOWL

I love everything about this bowl: The chewy, hearty grains; the warm, tender greens; a savory herb dressing; and a gorgeous, sunny-side up egg that gushes golden, buttery goodness over everything that gets in its way.

SWEET POTATOES

2 small sweet potatoes

½ cup plus 4 tablespoons extra virgin olive oil

FARRO, WILD RICE, OR FREEKEH

½ cup uncooked farro, wild rice, or freekeh (whole or cracked)

1 cup water

Maldon sea salt

KALE

1 cup chopped kale

DRESSING

1 cup organic plain whole-milk kefir

1 tablespoon chopped fresh flat-leaf parsley

2 tablespoons lemon juice or sherry vinegar

SUNNY-SIDE UP EGGS

4 large brown eggs

FOR SERVING

One 16-ounce can black beans, drained

½ cup diced Heirloom tomatoes (red, yellow, green), plus extra for garnish

FOR THE SWEET POTATOES Preheat the oven to 450°F.

Rub the sweet potatoes with 1 tablespoon of the olive oil, then wrap them in foil and roast until a small knife easily pierces the sweet potato, about 20 minutes. When cool enough to handle, cut them into ½-inch-thick slices.

FOR THE FARRO, WILD RICE, OR FREEKEH

In a rice cooker: Combine your chosen grain with the water, 1 tablespoon of the olive oil, and 1 pinch of the sea salt. Cook according to the rice cooker instructions.

On the stovetop: In a saucepan, combine your chosen grain with the water, 1 table-spoon the olive oil, and 1 pinch of the salt and bring to a soft boil. Reduce to a simmer, cover, and cook over low heat until done, about 45 minutes for farro, wild rice and whole freekeh; 20 minutes for cracked freekeh.

FOR THE KALE *While the grains and sweet potatoes are cooking . . .*

In a medium sauté pan, heat 1 tablespoon of the olive oil over medium-high heat. Add the kale and sauté until soft, 3 to 4 minutes. (Add a small amount of water if the kale begins to stick or turn too brown.) Season with a pinch of salt and set aside.

FOR THE DRESSING In a bowl, whisk together the kefir, parsley, ½ cup olive oil, a pinch of salt, and the lemon juice. Set aside.

FOR THE SUNNY-SIDE UP EGGS In the same pan as the kale, cook the eggs in the remaining 1 tablespoon olive oil to sunny-side up perfection, seasoning with sea salt toward the end.

TO PLATE Place the sautéed kale in a wide, deep bowl. Sprinkle with black beans, cooked grains, tomatoes, and sweet potato. Drizzle with the dressing, then slide the eggs on top before enjoying.

CHEF'S TIP Double or triple this recipe (except for the eggs) and you can enjoy this dish throughout the week, cooking the eggs just before plating.

Smoked Trout Marinated in Kefir with Arugula Salad

In the '90s, my parents owned a popular Russian supper club in the Chicago suburbs called *Moscow Nights*. We featured live music—famous Russian singers backed by their bands and playing everything from Top 40 hits (George Michael's "Careless Whisper" and anything by ABBA comes to mind) to old classics like "I Will Survive" and "Sunny" by Boney M. . . . though my dad was known to hop onstage and sing "Livin' la Vida Loca" karaoke-style, too. People would arrive at 8 p.m. with twenty to 200 of their closest friends and stay until three in the morning. I think that because Russians and Ukrainians have historically experienced so much tragedy and pain, when there's an opportunity to celebrate, we celebrate. Turning forty-three? Time to party! It's a Sunday night? Nostrovia! All of my and my brother's birthdays, my parents' anniversaries—we gathered at Moscow Nights for everything. I even worked as a hostess there throughout college, every Friday and Saturday night and every Sunday brunch.

Going to a Russian restaurant isn't a quick, in-and-out kind of thing. It's an experience. Every table is blanketed with multiple bottles of vodka and dozens of dishes: Pickled vegetables, a variety of mayonnaise-based salads, caviar, blinis, piroshkis (small fried dumplings filled with savory meat or vegetables) and shimmery, head-on smoked fish. To the uninitiated, the spread could seem intimidating. But for a group of people who emigrated here from a place and time characterized by breadlines and empty grocery store shelves, the food tasted divine, abundant, and opulent.

To be honest, smoked trout took a while to grow on me. As a young girl, I didn't love looking at a fish on the table and feeling like it was looking back at me. But this particular recipe is deconstructed, and the creamy kefir marinade balances the fish's briny flavor. Served over peppery arugula, it will wake up your taste buds.

PROBIOTIC POWER

Guests who tossed back vodka shots at Moscow Nights until 2 a.m. knew that kefir is a near-guaranteed Russian hangover remedy. Coincidence, or divine intervention?

SERVES 4

¾ pound smoked trout or whitefish (whole fillet, skin-on)

¾ cup organic plain whole-milk kefir

2 tablespoons chopped chives

2 tablespoons sliced red onion

Juice of 1 lemon, plus wedges for garnish

¼ cup extra virgin olive oil

2 pinches Maldon sea salt

6 ounces arugula

Place the trout in a glass storage container. In a bowl, mix the kefir, chives, and red onion and pour over the trout. Seal the container and marinate in the refrigerator for 2 hours or, preferably, overnight.

Gently remove the trout from the storage container and set aside. Pour the kefir mixture out of the container into a bowl. Stir in the lemon juice, olive oil, and salt until fully combined. Divide the arugula among four plates, dressing it with the kefir dressing, then top each salad with 3 ounces of trout (about one-quarter of the fish), gently moving back the skin and pulling the fish away from the bones.

FISH FOR BREAKFAST?

It's not as odd as it sounds. The Japanese typically start their day with salmon, rice, miso, and vegetables; in Britain, it's smoked kippers; stateside, bagel, lox, and cream cheese is a classic brunch combination. Fish, especially oily fish like trout, salmon, and sardines, makes for a surprisingly smart breakfast; rich in cognition-enhancing omega-3 fatty acids, a recent study linked eating baked or broiled (not fried) fish once a week with larger gray matter in regions of the brain responsible for memory. The protein and healthy fats are sure to keep you full until lunch, too.

Big Easy Pumpkin Beignets

New Orleans holds a special place in my heart. This city doesn't just ooze culture—it bleeds, sweats, and cries it. NOLA is a nonstop blitz of color, noise, and language. From the soulful tunes of Jazz Fest to the debauchery of Bourbon Street . . . crazy costumes, daily parades, endless beads at Mardis Gras . . . storybook French Quarter courtyard weddings . . . music emanating from every corner . . . cuisine featuring Cajun, Creole, French, and African influences . . . and a wildly diverse mishmash of characters, ethnicities, and heritages.

Every building has a story, like a movie set that's come to life. Take the local dry cleaners I visit when I'm down there. One hundred years ago, it was a woman's hospital. Flores, the owner, outlived her four business partners. In sixty-nine years, she's never missed a day of work, and every day, for nearly three-quarters of a century, she sits on the same stool, using a pen and paper to keep track of her business. No computers. Same stool. Sometimes she reminds me of my father, who also liked to run his business with a pen and paper. I bring her coffee and share my beignets with her.

Meanwhile, local artist Mrs. Jesse, who once held a funeral for Barbie, never sits down. She's always on the go; walking and walking. No one knows where Miss Jesse is going, but she's clearly on a mission.

You can wander over to Royal Street to have a custom poem written for you by Cubs the Poet, typed out on an old-fashioned typewriter. Catch some local street performers. (Darth Vader belting out pop hits especially puts a smile on my face.) Get your retail therapy fix at KREWE, for locally designed sunnies with names like Dauphine and Louisa and a quick shot of espresso. Or check out a graffiti street art installation in the Bywater neighborhood by activist Cleo Wade.

I'm also drawn to New Orleans's spirit of resiliency. So much suffering has unraveled here that you can practically see the stories radiating from its walls. But out of that suffering, incredible art, music, and cuisine have been born. I can't help but feel inspired when I'm there; that's why much of The Kefir Cookbook *was written in this legendary city.*

At least once a year I like to have a tarot card reading in the gardens of Jackson Square, then treat myself to a beignet at Café Du Monde on the Mississippi River. Okay, maybe two. Beignets are square pieces of dough, fried and then bathed in powdered sugar. They're the opposite of organic, whole food . . . but hey, at least they're local! This pumpkin recipe is my attempt to inject a little homegrown Illinois flavor into these French-style doughnuts. Laissez les bons temps rouler.

1 package active dry yeast

½ cup very hot water

Pinch of kosher salt

2½ cups whole wheat flour

3 large brown eggs

1 tablespoon cooking oil (peanut, grapeseed, or coconut)

1 cup canned pumpkin puree

¼ cup organic plain whole-milk kefir

Vegetable oil, for deep-frying (I use a mix of grapeseed and peanut oil)

½ cup powdered sugar

Dissolve the yeast in the hot water with the kosher salt. Combine the dissolved yeast with 1 cup of the flour and mix until smooth. Form the yeast/flour mixture into a ball and place in a large bowl. Cover the bowl with a kitchen towel and set in a warm place until doubled in size, about 1 hour.

Use a fork to beat the eggs until frothy. Add the remaining 1½ cups flour and the cooking oil, mixing well with a wooden spoon or whisk.

Once the yeast/flour mixture has doubled in size, combine it with the egg/flour mixture. Stir in the pumpkin puree and kefir and mix until completely smooth. Let stand for 1 hour. The dough should be elastic and spring back when stretched.

Pour 1½ inches vegetable oil into a deep, straight-sided frying pan and heat the oil to 360°F. (You can test the temperature by dropping in a small amount of the batter. If it immediately starts to bubble and float, the temperature is correct.) Using a soup spoon or a large tablespoon, drop spoonfuls of dough into the hot oil. Fry until golden brown, about 1 minute per side. Use the spoon to baste the cooking dough with a bit of oil as they fry. Drain the beignets on paper towels, then use a small sieve to dust them with powdered sugar.

Dark Chocolate Chip Zucchini Muffins

If you enjoy carrot cake or pumpkin bread, then you know that baking with veggies can yield some magical results. Here, grated zucchini bakes up almost impossibly tender and moist. Using coconut oil in place of butter adds a shot of lauric acid (helpful for raising good cholesterol levels); and because honey has a slightly higher amount of fructose than sugar, it tastes sweeter, but less is needed. Finally, the smattering of chocolate chips adds just the right amount of decadence. Our daughters like to bake these on their birthdays, and bring them to school to share with the class. The kids don't care that the zucchini is giving them a dose of manganese for optimum brain functioning, antioxidants lutein and zeaxanthin for healthy vision, and filling fiber. All they know is that when they bite into their muffin, they're greeted with a constellation of mini chocolate chips and festive green confetti.

SERVES 6

ZUCCHINI
2 cups shredded unpeeled zucchini (using a box grater or mandolin)
½ teaspoon plus 1 pinch kosher salt

MUFFINS
2 cups whole wheat flour
1 teaspoon ground Saigon cinnamon
½ teaspoon baking soda
½ teaspoon baking powder
2 large brown eggs
¼ cup coconut oil, melted and cooled, plus more for greasing the pan
1 cup organic plain whole-milk kefir
½ cup honey
1 teaspoon vanilla extract
⅓ cup mini semisweet chocolate chips

FOR THE ZUCCHINI Place the shredded zucchini into a small bowl and sprinkle 1 pinch of kosher salt over the top, gently mixing it in by hand. Set aside for 1 hour. After that, use your hands to squeeze out any excess water and set the zucchini on a paper towel to drain further.

FOR THE MUFFINS Preheat the oven to 375°F.

In a bowl, mix together the flour, cinnamon, baking soda, baking powder, and ½ teaspoon kosher salt. In a separate bowl, beat the eggs with a fork or whisk until fully beaten, then add the melted coconut oil, kefir, honey, and vanilla. Stir the egg mixture into the flour mixture and mix until smooth. Stir in the chocolate chips, then the zucchini, mixing until fully incorporated.

Grease 6 cups of a muffin tin with a little melted coconut oil. Fill each muffin cup to the top with batter. Bake until a knife stuck in the center of a muffin comes out clean, about 20 minutes.

CHEF'S TIP New to baking with zucchini? It can be substituted in most recipes that call for shredded carrots. Zucchini has more water than carrots, so your recipe will bake up softer, and the texture of the zucchini itself will disappear into the batter more.

NEED A GREAT END-OF-THE-YEAR TEACHER GIFT?

Pour the batter into a small metal loaf pan, sprinkle it with a light coating of sugar, and bake it at 375°F until a knife stuck in the center of the loaf comes out clean, about 20 minutes. Once cooled, wrap it in pretty cellophane and tie it with a raffia bow that has been looped through a piece of your child's artwork.

SMOOTHIES AND SMOOTHIE BOWLS

Most store-bought smoothies are full of sugar, fillers, and empty calories; juice and smoothie bars often rely on frozen yogurt, sherbet, or even ice cream for the dairy component. Add in some apple juice, maybe a frozen strawberry or two, and you've got a recipe for a sugar high, followed soon after by an energy crash.

Ready to give that smoothie a face-lift? Kefir supercharges smoothies with protein, calcium, and probiotics, turning them into high-quality, functional MVPs of breakfast: Delicious, hydrating, nourishing, filling, and they come together in a flash. Even better, the drinkable recipes on the following pages are loaded with nutrients, helping you nail your daily fruit and vegetable quota in one sitting. Think of them as a tastier, easier-to-swallow multivitamin.

Thick, cool, drinkable kefir is smoothie-esque all by itself, so it makes sense that kefir and smoothies so often go hand in hand. Still, the same old banana-spinach-berry combo can start to feel a little boring. These recipes will take you beyond the basic, bringing in fresh flavor combinations like pear and tart cherry; kale, avocado, lemon, and Himalayan pink salt; and hazelnut butter and cacao powder. There's even a mango, chocolate, and cricket (yes, cricket) blend that delivers more protein than an egg, but goes down like dessert.

Smoothies are ideal for rushed mornings when you want something healthier than coffee and a banana—sometimes I'll even make mine the night before, stash it in a mason jar in the fridge, and just give it a good shake before heading out the door.

But if you have the time to sit down and enjoy your creation, I urge you to give my smoothie bowls a try. It's just what it sounds like—a smoothie in a bowl—but when you top it with your favorite combination of fruit and crunch, the result is, without fail, a standout.

KID-FRIENDLY, EVERYONE-APPROVED

Smoothies are super child-friendly and perfect for picky eaters; most of them are naturally sweet (but sneakily infused with vitamins and minerals) and they basically taste like ice cream or sherbet. Keep your freezer stocked with an array of frozen fruits and invite your little ones to choose their favorites. You can also get creative making fun topping art on their smoothie bowls—think silly fruit faces, hearts, rainbows . . .

Purple Haze Smoothie

This jewel-hued beauty was inspired by the sun-drenched lavender fields of Provence in southeastern France, and the calming spell they put on me—hence the nod to Jimi Hendrix in the name of this dish. Known for its stress-relieving, sleep-enhancing benefits, lavender has a slightly sweet, floral flavor (its spikes and leaves can be used as a refreshing substitute for rosemary) and it loves being mixed with dairy and honey. Make this smoothie on days when tensions and stress are running high.

Blueberries add memory-enhancing antioxidants proven to slow cognitive decline, slash heart attack risk, and even stave off Alzheimer's and Parkinson's disease.

When baking or cooking with lavender, remember: A little goes a long way. Experiment with smaller amounts at first, adding more for a stronger floral flavor. Before adding it to the blender, be sure to bring it to your nose and deeply inhale.

1 cup organic plain whole-milk kefir

1 cup frozen blueberries, plus extra for garnish

1 cup frozen blackberries, plus extra for garnish

1 small frozen banana, peeled

2 tablespoons honey

1 tablespoon chopped fresh lavender

Pinch of sea salt or Himalayan pink salt

In a blender, combine all ingredients and blend until you achieve your desired consistency. Garnish with extra frozen berries.

CHEF'S TIPS

Always use *culinary lavender*, which differs from the type used in beauty products; find it at higher-end markets, apothecaries, and online.

Brown bananas are perfect for smoothies . . . extra sweet. Peel them before freezing so you'll always have them on hand when a smoothie craving hits.

When you top a smoothie with frozen berries, the slightly warmer temperature of the smoothie causes the berries to thaw ever so slightly; they look like they're covered with frosty crystals or powdered sugar.

DID YOU KNOW . . .

English farmers would stash lavender flowers inside their hats to prevent headaches after long days of working in the heat.

Blue Algae Superfood Smoothie Bowl

Trust me: You want this smoothie bowl in your life.

Its power comes from blue-green algae (BGA), considered one of the most nutrient-dense foods on the planet. Like kefir, BGA has a storied ancient history; humans have been consuming it as food or medicine as far back as fifth-century China and fourteenth-century Aztec civilization. It contains a bioactive component called phycocyanin, a natural pigment believed to have antiaging and antioxidant properties. Several studies have demonstrated BGA's antiviral, antitumor, anti-inflammatory, antidiabetic, antiallergenic, and cholesterol-lowering effects. This popular smoothie mix-in is also packed with essential amino acids (the building blocks of proteins) and fiber, along with carotenoids and plant sterols—associated with a reduced risk of cardiovascular disease and cholesterol, respectively.

Because BGA grows in the ocean, it has a mildly briny taste, but mixed with strongly flavored fruits like pineapple and blueberries, you won't notice it. Get ready for the superfood of the future—the ultimate green machine.

SERVES 1

1 cup frozen pineapple chunks

1 cup frozen blueberries

¾ cup organic plain whole-milk kefir

½ teaspoon vanilla extract

½ cup coconut or hemp milk

2 tablespoons light agave syrup

2 tablespoons lemon juice

2 tablespoons blue-green algae powder (I like E3Live's Blue Majik or Zhou Nutrition's non-GMO spirulina)

1 tablespoon grated fresh ginger

Pinch of sea salt or Himalayan pink salt

SUGGESTED TOPPINGS (2 TABLESPOONS EACH)

Kiwi slices

Almond slices

Fresh blueberries

Sunflower seeds

Edible flowers

In a blender, combine all ingredients and blend until you achieve your desired consistency. Pour the smoothie into a bowl and top with your favorite toppings.

Christy's Mother Runner Smoothie

RECIPE COURTESY OF CHRISTY TURLINGTON BURNS

"I never thought of myself as a runner. I was always drawn to yoga; running seemed too harsh, too much pounding on my bones. Yet today, I am proud to call myself a runner! I've finished six marathons, a bunch more half-marathons, and running has become yet another form of meditation and purpose for me.

"Julie inspired me to run my first marathon. We met in 2010, when Julie was pregnant with Misha. I had just launched my maternal health nonprofit, Every Mother Counts (EMC), with the goal of making pregnancy and childbirth safe for every mother, everywhere. When I gave birth to my daughter in 2003, I experienced a postpartum hemorrhage. Before then I was not aware that hundreds of thousands of girls and women die every year bringing life into the world and that 98 percent of those deaths were preventable. Once I learned this, I felt compelled to do something, to try to make an impact and help prevent these senseless deaths. I traveled to Tanzania, Bangladesh, Guatemala, and parts of the US to direct and produce the documentary No Woman, No Cry, highlighting the maternal health challenges felt by millions of girls and women around the globe. Julie and I bonded over pregnancy talk, and I asked her to join me on a trip to Bangladesh the following summer to screen No Woman, No Cry and experience the impact of our work on the ground firsthand

"On a long, bumpy drive along the chaotic streets of Dhaka, Julie mentioned how much she loved running marathons. At that point, I had never run farther than six miles—I was more of a yogi. Shortly thereafter, Every Mother Counts was offered a few slots at the New York City Marathon. At first, I said, 'Sure, we can find people to run for us.' But the more I thought about it, the more I started to realize that I wanted to do this myself. In so many parts of the world, 5K is the minimum distance a pregnant woman needs to walk if she wants to deliver in a medical center or hospital with skilled providers; it is feasible that a woman would need to travel 26 miles to reach a hospital for emergency obstetric care. I wanted to run 26.2 miles to raise awareness and money and galvanize our community in the hopes that other women wouldn't have to face distance as a barrier to accessing essential health care.

"I asked Julie if she would run NYC with me (she said yes), and I committed myself to four months of training. At first, it was daunting; but after I passed the ten-mile benchmark, I began to pick up confidence. Soon enough, I found myself thinking, 'Running might be my sport!'

"Julie and I have run three marathons together so far. She also turned me on to kefir, and now that's one of my favorite post-run recovery snacks. It's got protein, calcium, and other restorative properties to help counteract all that pavement pounding, and it tastes so refreshing and cool going down. I like to blend my kefir into a smoothie with frozen fruit, almond butter, and coconut water. (Julie and I also partnered to produce a special low-fat blueberry kefir, with portions of the proceeds going to Every Mother Counts.) The orange flowers in this smoothie evoke EMC's Orange Rose, the symbol that we feel represents a beautiful, vibrant, and strong life, like that of a mother who has been supported throughout pregnancy and childbirth. It is a powerful reminder that safer motherhood is possible."

Christy Turlington Burns is a mother, the founder and CEO of the nonprofit organization Every Mother Counts, director/producer of the documentary film *No Woman, No Cry*, and the author of *Living Yoga: Creating a Life Practice*.

Training with Christy Turlington Burns for a marathon in Laguna Beach, California.

1 cup organic vanilla kefir

1 small frozen banana, peeled

2 ounces firmly packed baby spinach

1 cup frozen pineapple chunks

½ cup creamy almond butter

¼ cup coconut water

½ tablespoon grated fresh ginger

Pinch of sea salt or Himalayan pink salt

Orange flowers (or an orange slice), for garnish

In a blender, combine all ingredients and blend until you achieve your desired consistency. For optimal recovery, enjoy it about 30 minutes postworkout.

STEP-SAVER Pinched for time post-run? A glass of kefir and a banana will do the trick.

DID YOU KNOW . . .

You don't have to be a runner to benefit from this smoothie, which has iron-rich spinach and heart-healthy fats from the almond butter. But athletes will appreciate the pineapple's antioxidants, which help neutralize the free radicals created by exercise, as well as the slightly peppery ginger's soothing impact on postexercise muscle soreness. The protein helps with muscle repair, plus kefir has the perfect ratio of carbohydrates, protein, and other nutrients needed for energy and optimum performance. Long-distance runners may especially benefit from the immune-boosting elements, as extended runs can be hard on your system.

Nutella Smoothie

Summer of 1976: My family and I had emigrated from the former Soviet Union but had not yet reached America. The Hebrew Immigrant Aid Society, a refugee agency, set us up in transitional housing in Rome, where we lived for three months while awaiting the paperwork and green cards that would allow us to enter the United States. My parents arrived with one suitcase, no money, no sense of what was to come.

While we were in Rome, my mother discovered Nutella, a creamy hazelnut-cocoa spread that symbolizes everything the Soviet Union was not: Pleasure, decadence, delight. We couldn't afford our own jar, but crepe shops would occasionally offer my mom free tastes. To her, those bites were mini escapes, edible dreams. Less than four years later, my mom became one of the first American importers of Nutella, negotiating exclusive deals with the original owners. (She named her company JE International, after my brother, Eddie, and me, Julie.)

A rare photograph of my family taken from our time in Rome while we were in exile waiting for our papers to authorize our arrival into the United States.

My family and I revisiting the Hotel Pensione Maxim in Rome when I was in high school. This was the housing facility we called home for three months when we were exiled in 1976.

This recipe is my homage to Rome, melding hazelnuts and cashews with intensely flavored cacao powder. It's sweet, thick, nutty, and tastes sinful . . . but I promise it's full of protein, healthy fats, and American Dreams.

When I visit Rome now, I can't imagine how my parents must have felt, arriving from the closed-off Soviet Union, characterized by so much scarcity, to a cosmopolitan city full of food, fashion, and entrepreneurism. As I watch my own girls wander down the cobblestone streets, Italians smiling at them and calling them piccolo bambino, I can feel my father with us. So much gratitude for this city that warmly welcomed us over forty years ago. My heart belongs to Rome. Ciao.

SERVES 1

1 cup organic plain whole-milk kefir

½ cup hazelnut butter (if not available, substitute creamy toasted almond butter)

¼ cup cacao powder

½ cup chopped pitted Medjool dates

Pinch of sea salt or Himalayan pink salt

In a blender, combine all ingredients and blend until you achieve your desired consistency.

Goddess Kefir Smoothie Bowl

There are museums out there for everything: A Money Museum in Chicago. A UFO Museum in Roswell, New Mexico. There's even the International Banana Museum in Mecca, California. But you know what museum doesn't yet exist? A museum for women. No, not a single museum in the world is dedicated solely to the history of women and their epic contributions to society—women who fought for the right to vote, women involved in the Civil Rights Movement, women in arts, women in STEAM fields, women in politics. I mean, I like bananas as much as the next person, but the fact that, in this day and age, there is no centralized location shining a light on the achievements of women is embarrassing, and it's shameful.

As part of the effort to create a National Women's History Museum, Lifeway helped organize a Women Making History brunch in Los Angeles. Businesswomen, politicians, and dedicated changemakers like Hillary Clinton and Laura Bush, Molly Simms, Tracee Ellis Ross, Rachel Zoe, and Abigail Breslin have joined in as we strategize ways to build the first ever national museum dedicated exclusively to the contributions of women. At this annual Women Making History brunch, we served a chilled breakfast soup that proved perfect for the occasion: Elegant, light, sophisticated. I nicknamed it the Goddess Smoothie Bowl, because to me, all women are goddesses. We used kefir not only to deliver a cool, creamy consistency, but to enrich their breakfasts with satiating protein and immune-boosting probiotics—both come in handy when you're trying to move mountains.

SERVES 1

1 cup organic plain whole-milk kefir

1 cup frozen mixed berries

1 cup loosely packed spinach

1 small frozen banana, peeled

½ avocado, pitted and peeled

½ cup chopped lacinato (Tuscan) kale

1 teaspoon spirulina

2 tablespoons creamy toasted almond butter

Orange segments, for garnish

Roasted sunflower seeds

Roasted nuts

Cacao nibs

Unsweetened coconut flakes

Fresh berries

Hemp seeds

In a blender, combine all ingredients and blend until you achieve your desired consistency. Pour the smoothie into a bowl and top with your favorite toppings. Garnish with orange segments.

Cricket Smoothie

You'll be crossing "Eat crickets" off your edible Bucket List soon.

Don't believe me? Entomologists love crickets and other insects for their impressive amounts of sustainable, environmentally friendly, meat-free protein, and magnesium. Food trend experts project the edible-insect industry will be worth more than $360 million in the next few years.

This smoothie recipe spontaneously happened while hanging out with my good friend Katrina Markoff, founder of the amazing Vosges Haut-Chocolat. Katrina manages to pair her chocolate with exotic ingredients like ginger and wasabi, fennel and absinthe, or sweet Indian curry, so I wasn't surprised to see a bag of cricket flour in her pantry. As fate would have it, my daughters—already totally intrigued by bugs—had just returned from a visit to the local nature museum, where they'd had the chance to sample dried crickets. We began dabbling, blending frozen mangoes with Katrina's super-dark cocoa and two kinds of bugs: kefir's good-for-you probiotics and a pinch of cricket powder. Our kids couldn't get enough.

SERVES 1

1 cup organic plain whole-milk kefir

1 cup frozen mango chunks

½ cup coconut milk

2 ounces Vosges Haut-Chocolat Coconut Ash & Banana Super Dark chocolate (or any dark chocolate with at least 70% cacao) or 1 ounce cacao powder)

2 tablespoons cricket powder (I like Exo and Chirp brands)

Pinch of sea salt or Himalayan pink salt

Small handful blueberries, for garnish (optional)

Small handful microgreens, for garnish (optional)

In a blender, combine all ingredients except the blueberries and microgreens and blend until you achieve your desired consistency.

SPOOKY SMOOTHIE

Delight your little goblins on Halloween by rebranding this "Bugs 'n' Sludge" or "Creepy Crawler Smoothie," and telling them there are not one, but two types of bugs blended inside! (Crickets and probiotics.)

CHEF'S TIP On its own, cricket flour has a subtly nutty, earthy flavor, but all you'll notice in this recipe is mango, coconut, and chocolate.

Vitamin C Cure Smoothie Bowl

You already know that the probiotics in kefir can supercharge your immunity; science has demonstrated over and over that good-for-you gut bugs play a critical role in guarding and protecting your GI tract, Ground Zero of the immune system, from disease-causing bacteria. Combine that effect with vitamin C and you have a recipe for feeling good.

But the star vitamin of this smoothie bowl is good for so much more than getting rid of sniffles. Our bodies need vitamin C to produce collagen (for plump skin), to aid in wound healing, to synthesize vital brain neurotransmitters, and more. It helps us better absorb the iron from our beans and leafy greens, making it a must for vegetarians and vegans. Because it limits the damaging effects of free radicals, scientists believe vitamin C may help prevent or delay the development of heart disease and certain cancers, plus studies link it with reducing high blood pressure, chronic inflammation, and ulcers.

In addition to the C-rich fruits in this bowl, camu-camu berry power adds an extra jolt of nutrition. Amazonian camu-camu berries are one of the world's richest sources of vitamin C—they contain sixty times more per serving than an orange—and just a single teaspoon surpasses your daily needs. When dried and crushed, the resulting reddish-orange powder lends this recipe a tart berry flavor that's balanced by the sweetness of the cantaloupe and honeydew.

SERVES 1

3/4 cup organic plain whole-milk kefir

1/2 cup fresh orange juice

1 cup fresh or frozen honeydew chunks

1 cup fresh or frozen cantaloupe chunks

1 cup frozen butternut squash chunks

2 tablespoons honey

1 teaspoon camu-camu berry powder

1/4 cup grated fresh turmeric

1/4 cup grated fresh ginger

Pinch of sea salt or Himalayan pink salt

SUGGESTED TOPPINGS (2 TABLESPOONS EACH)

Orange segments

Kiwi slices

Raisins

Chopped nuts: almonds, walnuts, pecans, cashews, or peanuts

Toasted seeds: sesame, hemp, or sunflower

Fresh blueberries

Goji berries

Dusting of ground Espelette pepper

In a blender, combine all ingredients and blend until you achieve your desired consistency. Pour the smoothie into a bowl and top with your favorite toppings.

CHEF'S TIP What's Espelette pepper? Also called *piment d'Espelette*, this bright red, smoky chili pepper wakes up the flavor in food. (It's killer on watermelon with a little sea salt and lime.) You can get it at most spice stores; if not, substitute smoked paprika.

Banana, Date, and Hemp Smoothie

Wanna bliss out? Take a sip: This mystic smoothie is overflowing with the relaxation mineral magnesium. Creamy, slightly nutty hemp milk is a bit thicker than other alt-milks, and while it won't get you buzzed (hemp seeds come from the same Cannabis sativa plant as marijuana but don't contain the psychoactive chemical THC), it will give you a health high. Hemp milk contains essential fatty acids, anti-inflammatory vitamin E, and many brands are fortified with vitamin D and calcium. And kefir itself may help you mellow out . . . in animal studies, feeding mice probiotics increases the levels of GABA, a neurotransmitter with Valium-like effects; young adults who consume more fermented foods experience fewer symptoms of social anxiety. Get ready to chill out and unwind.

SERVES 1

1 cup organic plain whole-milk kefir

1 small frozen banana

½ cup hemp milk

½ cup chopped pitted Medjool dates

1 tablespoon hemp seeds

1 tablespoon vanilla extract

Pinch of ground cinnamon, plus extra for garnish

Pinch of sea salt or Himalayan pink salt

1 tablespoon peanut butter, for garnish

In a blender, combine all ingredients except the peanut butter and blend until you achieve your desired consistency. Garnish with cinnamon and the peanut butter.

PROBIOTIC POWER

Bananas, which are prebiotics, are known to help maintain harmony among the microbes residing in your GI tract; maybe that's why bananas are thought to help soothe an upset stomach.

The Amazebowl

Many of the recipes in this book were inspired by my travels or life experiences, or are modern takes on family favorites. But some, like the Amazebowl, exist solely for one reason: They taste insane.

I knew I wanted a smoothie bowl version of the green juice I so love; something filling and not too sweet. The result is a smoothie bowl that's saturated with nutrition and flavor. The avocado makes the smoothie base extraordinarily silky, and somehow, even though there's no banana or pineapple to be found in this recipe, it has a slight hint of the tropical. In fact, when I was finalizing the ingredients list, I invited a few friends over to sample it; more than one of them noticed the surprising but very subtle banana flavor, announcing, "That's amazing." Hence the name Amazebowl.

Because it's only slightly sweet (thanks to a touch of light agave syrup), you can amp up the toppings to make it go savory or sweet, depending on your palate or mood.

SERVES 1

½ cup chopped lacinato (Tuscan) kale leaves, center ribs removed

1 cup firmly packed chopped baby spinach

1 medium avocado, pitted and peeled

½ cup organic plain whole-milk kefir

1 tablespoon light agave syrup

2 tablespoons cold water

2 tablespoons lemon juice

Pinch of sea salt or Himalayan pink salt

SUGGESTED TOPPINGS (2 TABLESPOONS EACH)

Avocado slices

Chopped dates

Hard-boiled egg slices

Chopped olives

Seeds or nuts (your favorite)

Orange segments and peel

Drizzle of olive oil

In a blender, combine all ingredients and blend until you achieve your desired consistency. Pour the smoothie into a bowl and top with your favorite toppings.

CHEF'S TIP There's no ice in this recipe to keep it cold—and it tastes its best when chilled—so I recommend having your toppings prepped and ready to go before starting.

Jet Lag Recovery Smoothie

In Gloria Steinem's My Life on the Road, *the passionate feminist relays the lessons she's learned through countless days of travel. Steinem is a dedicated lifelong wanderer—she's been around the world, organizing women on US college campuses and in foreign countries, raising awareness at voting booths and presidential rallies, hosting community-wide talking circles, and more. That wandering, she writes, has shaped her into the activist and political organizer she is to this day. (She's in her early eighties.) All that time logged on planes and trains, in taxis and rickshaws, has yielded countless stories, many of them emotional, thought provoking, and unexpectedly profound. Maybe that's why she doesn't have a driver's license: Without one, she writes, "adventure starts the moment I leave my door."*

Like Steinem, I travel a lot and jet lag comes with the territory—and while I feel it's a reasonable price to pay for the rewards of travel, symptoms like insomnia and dehydration are no fun. This hydrating pick-me-up is my secret weapon. Tart cherries are rich in the sleep-regulating hormone melatonin, known to help people suffering from insomnia and travel-related sleep troubles. Banana offers potassium and magnesium for relaxation, and pears add a dose of easily digestible fiber that acts like a sponge as it travels through the digestive tract, absorbing toxins. (Hello, airplane air!) Even if you're not traveling, drinking this smoothie in the afternoon or evening can help you sleep more peacefully.

Gloria, this one's for you.

SERVES 1

1 cup organic plain whole-milk kefir

1 small frozen banana, peeled

1 cup fresh pear chunks

½ cup tart cherry juice

2 tablespoons flaxseeds (ground or whole)

In a blender, combine all ingredients and blend until you achieve your desired consistency.

PROBIOTIC POWER

Travel may be nourishing to the soul, but it can take a toll on your body. Many people experience GI troubles when they're in a new environment and eating different foods. Drinking kefir and eating fermented foods before, during, and after your trip can help you build a strong, resilient gut from the get-go, offering you an added layer of protection from the moment you step on that plane. Think of probiotics as travel insurance!

Elie Metchnikoff was the first scientist to study the effect of kefir on the body. He was awarded the 1908 Nobel Prize for his theory that the longevity of people in the northern Caucasus who lived past the age of one hundred was due to the lactic acid bacteria found in fermented milk.

Mango Bazaar Lassi

Walking down the streets of Mumbai, you can't help but feel overwhelmed by the intensity of it all—people shouting in Hindi, Bengali, or a half-dozen other languages; horns blaring as cars and motorbikes pass by way too closely; children giggling, mantras being chanted. Your eyes dance from the roadside spice stalls—vibrant with golden yellow turmeric, coriander, black cardamom pods, deep red saffron threads, and glossy green curry leaves—to women dressed in fuchsia, purple, and orange saris, glimmering bangles piled up both wrists. Walking a single block might take five minutes, as you navigate the street vendors, rickshaws, bicycles (built for one but carrying three), and the occasional cow.

Lassi is a traditional Indian beverage, a blend of yogurt, spices, water, and occasionally fruit. The smoothie-esque drink dates back six thousand years, when it was enjoyed as a thirst quencher to combat the heat of South Asia. Lassi is sold on every street corner in India and is widely available throughout the Indian subcontinent. (They even have lassi vending machines at the airports and train stations.) On my first day in Mumbai, I wandered the spice stalls, sampled goat curry and dal puri (fried, puffed bread), and took an outdoor yoga class, cooling off afterward with fresh mango lassi.

SERVES 1

1 cup frozen mango chunks

1 cup organic plain whole-milk kefir

Pinch of Maldon sea salt

1 teaspoon chopped fresh mint

1 tablespoon toasted coconut flakes

In a blender, combine the mango, kefir, and salt and blend until completely smooth. Pour into a pint glass and top with the chopped mint and coconut.

Almond and Toasted Coconut Soothing Smoothie Bowl

Some of the most exciting new research to emerge around the benefits of probiotics has to do with mental health. The gut acts as a second brain of sorts; a network of millions of neurons line our GI tract, connecting our bellies and our brains via a highway of hormones and chemicals. If you've ever felt butterflies in your stomach or successfully "followed your gut," you've experienced this second brain firsthand.

More and more research is shoring up this connection: Eating fermented foods like kefir, pickles, kombucha, and kimchi can reduce symptoms of social anxiety; and people who take probiotics may start their day with lower levels of cortisol—the stress hormone—in their saliva.

When you're enjoying this bowl, those neurons will be bathed in probiotics thanks to the creamy kefir. The trio of almond butter, almond milk, and chopped almonds delivers a hefty dose of zinc, a critical nutrient for maintaining a balanced mood. Don't forget the cacao nibs; also known as "nature's chocolate chips," cacao nibs contain many pleasure-inducing chemicals, including phenethylamine, which elicits the romantic love feelings you experience in the beginning of a new relationship, and anandamide, a compound whose name comes from ananda, *the Sanskrit word for "bliss."*

SERVES 1

¾ cup organic plain whole-milk kefir

½ cup creamy toasted almond butter

½ cup coconut manna or coconut butter

¼ cup unsweetened almond milk

Pinch of sea salt or Himalayan pink salt

1 tablespoon sliced almonds

2 tablespoons toasted coconut flakes

1 tablespoon cacao nibs

¼ cup baked butternut squash chunks

Pinch of ground cinnamon

Edible flowers (optional)

In a blender, combine the kefir, almond butter, coconut manna, almond milk, and salt and blend until you achieve your desired consistency. Pour the smoothie into a bowl, top with the almonds, coconut flakes, cacao nibs, and sweet potato chunks. Finish with a sprinkling of cinnamon and edible flowers (if using).

Julie's Kefir Bellini Smoothie

Enjoying a Bellini on the shore of the Grand Canal in Venice, Italy.

I became obsessed with Bellinis after sipping one while overlooking the Grand Canal on a trip to Venice. Traditionally comprising sparkling Prosecco blended with white peach puree, the brunch mainstay is said to have been born in the 1930s at Harry's Bar in Venice, Italy. (Giuseppe Cipriani, founder of that legendary drinking establishment, named his creation after Giovanni Bellini, an Italian Renaissance painter who no doubt knew how to enjoy a boozy brunch.)

For those times when Prosecco isn't an option (insert sad face here), it's still possible to capture the Bellini's essence of celebration through this smoothie mocktail, which uses kefir in place of sparkling Prosecco. Peaches love being mixed with anything creamy, and kefir's probiotics strains add a slight effervescence—it doesn't pack the same punch as Prosecco, but lingers subtly on the palate, letting the other flavors in this smoothie shine through. I like to throw in some mint leaf to add a little more tingle.

Red raspberries color this smoothie with a pretty pink blush. Try to use white peaches to give it a true Bellini vibe. I especially love picking fresh white peaches during the dog days of summer and making a pitcher of this frothy blend. Serve it in a champagne glass if you want to have some fun. Sip at your leisure.

SERVES 1

1 cup organic plain whole-milk kefir

1 cup frozen white peach slices

¼ cup aloe vera or cold water

¼ cup fresh raspberries

2 tablespoons honey

Pinch of sea salt or Himalayan pink salt

Mint leaves and raspberries, for garnish

DID YOU KNOW . . .

Thanks to its hint of effervescence, kefir is known throughout the beverage world as "the champagne of dairy."

In a blender, combine all ingredients and blend until you achieve your desired consistency.

SALADS, DRESSINGS, AND DIPS

If I could eat salad every day for the rest of my life, I would. Refreshing, thirst-quenching tomato-cucumber in the summer; warm, cozy sweet potato, quinoa, and goat cheese salad in the winter. I love the fresh ingredients, the chewy and crunchy toppings, the never-ending array of dressings to tie it all together. And I love that no matter how filling the fixings may be, you never finish a salad feeling weighed down or having buyer's remorse.

My passion for salads dates all the way back to my ancestors. Salads are a staple among Russians and Ukrainians, who historically have had to make do with very little, growing produce at their *dachas*, or summer homes, away from the smog and chaos of the city. My people have always treasured the freshness of the earth's bounty—my mom would excitedly gather the first prickly cucumbers and tiny, juicy tomatoes of the season from our backyard garden, the intense green aromas making her reminisce about tending to her own mother's garden decades earlier.

Attend a dinner at the home or restaurant of a Russian or Ukrainian and you can bet that more than half the dinner table will be covered in vegetable dishes of some form—fresh, marinated, pickled, and fermented. Funnily enough, hardly any Russian salads contain lettuce. Instead, they usually feature a hearty root vegetable or two as a base, like potatoes, beets, turnips, or carrots. You'll also likely find a plate of whole vegetables on the table—whole tomatoes, whole cucumbers, a whole green onion, nothing sliced—accompanied by a dish of salt. Guests pick their favorite one and just go to town, taking a bite of their cucumber or tomato as if it's a turkey leg, sprinkling salt on it as they go. The salt draws the liquid out of the veggies, intensifying their taste and rendering them almost impossibly juicy.

Thanks to vegetarian-friendly movements like Meatless Monday, the meat-as-a-condiment trend, and the rise in veggie-heavy restaurants, produce is getting the love it deserves these days. A good salad lives and dies by its dressing; you need a little fat, a little acid, a little salt, plus something to emulsify (bring together) all of the ingredients. Whole-milk kefir is a natural choice for a base; it has fat and acidity built right in, plus it works as an emulsifier, similar to egg or mustard. And because it's not heated, the probiotics stay alive and strong. It can replace buttermilk or yogurt in creamy dressings, or can be used to turn vinaigrettes creamy.

For similar reasons, kefir also works nicely in dips. Not only are dips flavorful and comforting, they're a sly way for vegetable avoiders (kids, especially) to get more produce into their system. Not even the most produce-reluctant among us can turn down my creamy, savory Kefir Labneh French Onion Dip (page 163); its ghee-fried onions are so addictive, no one will even notice all the crudités they're consuming in the process. And my Hummus (page 154) is like a gateway drug into the land of vegetables, opening the door to unlimited snacking on pepper strips, snap peas, grape tomatoes, and broccoli florets.

Ludmila's Russian Salad

It seems like every culture has a take on the tomato-and-cucumber salad—as the saying goes, "What grows together goes together." Throughout the Middle East, tomatoes and cukes are diced with onions and fresh parsley and served meze-style. In Greece, they dance with Kalamata olives and salty feta cheese. In Russia, they are prepared simply and humbly, with dill, sour cream, and lots of salt. My family's spin on this centuries-old favorite, of course, uses kefir as the salad dressing base.

This salad makes a bright, tasty accompaniment to grilled fish or meat—it pairs especially well with the Grilled Lamb Chops with Kefir Verde Sauce (page 269) or the Uzbek Shashlik (Kebabs) (page 230). You could also try it in the morning with your favorite simple egg dish, or save it for a healthy snack.

SERVES 4

2 cucumbers

1 tablespoon Maldon sea salt

1 pint cherry tomatoes, halved

1 tablespoon chopped fresh dill

¼ cup extra virgin olive oil

2 tablespoons organic plain whole-milk kefir

Black bread, for dunking

Peel the cucumbers, leaving thin strips of green skin. Halve lengthwise and remove seeds using a spoon. Slice the cucumbers on a slight bias and sprinkle with ½ tablespoon of the salt, allowing them to sit for at least 1 hour. Discard the cucumber liquid.

Sprinkle the cherry tomatoes with the remaining ½ tablespoon salt and combine with the salted cucumber, dill, and olive oil. Toss the mixture with the kefir and serve. (If you can wait, let the mixture sit for a few hours or overnight in the refrigerator, so the flavors can really meld.) Use the bread to sop up any leftover dressing.

MY FAVORITE SUMMER SNACK

Tomatoes scream *summer* to me—sun-warmed, juicy, mouthwatering. I'll load up my bag at the farmers' market with cherry, Roma, and heirloom tomatoes, snacking on some while we walk home. With simple recipes like this one, prime, seasonal ingredients are essential, so my recommendation is to only make this salad in the summer or fall, when tomatoes are perfectly, lusciously ripe. Besides intense flavor, you'll be maximizing the amount of nutrients you're getting . . . and tomatoes are standouts in this department. Tomatoes are one of the most potent food sources of lycopene, a well-researched free radical fighter. (Free radicals are misbehaving molecules that float throughout the body, damaging DNA in ways that can lead to cancer.) How potent? Research suggests that eating them may help offset the sun's damaging effects on skin—not enough to skip your sunblock, but every little bit helps. In this salad, the fat from the whole-milk kefir boosts your body's absorption of lycopene, while adding some staying power to an otherwise light dish. Tomatoes are also full of moisture—one medium tomato contains about two fluid ounces of water—so they're hydrating, making this a natural pick for summer dining.

End of Summer Massaged Kale and Pomegranate Salad

Hands down, summer is my favorite season. Beach trips. Boat rides. Tank tops and maxi dresses. Relaxing with friends and a crisp glass of rosé at a sidewalk café. High on vitamin D, the world is a happier place. As August winds down and autumn approaches, I sometimes feel a little melancholy, knowing that on just the other side, a brutal Chicago winter awaits. But then I think about all the great swag fall has to offer: Hay rides and s'mores. Tall boots and cozy sweaters. Apple picking. Hiking. Pumpkin-spiced anything.

Fall is the perfect time to celebrate the harvest. Yes, we say goodbye to sweet cherries and watermelon, but here come tart apples, juicy pears, and a cornucopia of colors and flavors of squash. Another hotly anticipated seasonal produce pick: pomegranates. The sweet-tart fruit is a true antioxidant powerhouse; one study found that pom juice has more antioxidants than red wine. Pomegranate seeds (arils) are perfect for layering in kefir parfaits, mixing into oatmeal and rice dishes, stirring into sauces and gremolatas, and bobbing in Prosecco and sangria. In this salad, pomegranate seeds add pops of sweetness; the acid from the kefir in the dressing tempers the slight bitterness of the kale.

Kale's no slouch in the nutrition department, either. One cup of raw, chopped kale surpasses your daily needs for vitamins A, C, and K; the fat from the kefir dressing enhances the bioavailability of these nutrients even more. The crinkly leafy green has bone-building calcium, copper, and iron—the latter two work together to help the body create energy-dispersing red blood cells. Because you're eating the kale raw, you'll maximize the amount of prebiotic fiber that makes its way to your GI tract, meaning extra fuel for the probiotics in the herbed kefir dressing.

DID YOU KNOW . . .

Some scholars believe it was not an apple, but a jewel-toned pomegranate that tempted Eve.

---

2 bunches baby kale

Pinch of Maldon sea salt

1 shallot, sliced crosswise

½ cup extra virgin olive oil

1 cup Basic Herbed Kefir Dressing (page 46)

1 cup pomegranate seeds (arils)

1 apple, cut into thin French fry–size sticks

1 pear, cut into thin French fry–size sticks

½ cup toasted almonds

1 cup small Thai or purple basil leaves, torn into bite-size pieces

Cut the kale as thinly as possible and place the shreds in a medium bowl. Sprinkle the kale with the salt, shallots, and olive oil. Massage the mixture into the kale and allow it to marinate for 1 hour. Toss the kale with the dressing, pomegranate seeds, apple, and pear sticks. Divide the salad among four salad plates, ensuring that each plate has an equal amount of fruit. Top each salad with the toasted almonds and torn basil leaves.

CHEF'S TIPS

Massaging the kale leaves before rinsing will tenderize them and release some of their natural bitter compounds, which will then wash away.

When selecting kale, look for smaller-leaved varieties; they're more tender and have a milder flavor. I like lacinato (Tuscan).

Punta Mita Catch of the Day Grilled Fish Salad with Kefir Cabbage Slaw and Baja Dressing

You know that feeling you get when you're on Day 2 of a five-day beach vacation, when your body and mind are utterly relaxed, the sound of lapping ocean waves fills your soul, and you realize, "I still have three more days of this left?" This dish is that feeling on a plate.

Our family started heading to Punta Mita, Mexico, in 2008, a few months after our first daughter, Leah, was born, and it's since evolved into a much-anticipated annual retreat. After a year of ninety-hour workweeks, perpetual business travel, school commitments, ballet, art and tennis lessons, and just the general craze of life, it's our opportunity to escape, unplug, refresh, and recharge. With the blizzards of the Windy City behind us, Punta Mita welcomes us with open arms and invites us to collapse into its thatched palapa-roof embrace.

Sun and surf are big draws, and as we watch our girls build sandcastles, snorkel, and chase iguanas, we order some food and refuel. Set amidst a backdrop of tropical flavors, the beach blossoms into a succulent paradise with the distinctive flavors and textures of regional Mexican cuisine—sweet corn, bright lime, spicy chipotle chilies, smoky tomatillo salsas, crumbly queso fresco. This Baja grilled fish salad with kefir slaw is the epitome of that: It has acidity, crunch, and a touch of creaminess from the Baja kefir dressing. And like many simple Mexican dishes, it's naturally healthy, easy to prepare, and guilt-free. I promise that one bite will transport you to a place where palm trees sway, waves crash, and the most important task on your agenda is "Build sandcastles." Time to kick back.

Note: Corona with lime is optional but highly recommended.

One of our favorite yearly traditions is to make tortillas with the cook at Rosa Mexicana in Punta Mita, Mexico.

SERVES 4 TO 6

FISH

1½ pounds mahi-mahi, halibut, or red snapper

1 shallot, minced

1 clove garlic, minced

3 tablespoons lemon or lime juice

1 teaspoon extra virgin olive oil

1 teaspoon Himalayan sea salt or kosher salt

SLAW

2 cups shredded red cabbage

2 cups shredded napa cabbage

2 cups shredded carrots

1 medium red onion, diced

½ cup chopped fresh cilantro

Juice of ½ lemon or lime

1 tablespoon Maldon sea salt

1 jalapeño, seeded and minced (optional; leave on the side if serving kids)

DRESSING

1 cup organic plain whole-milk kefir

Juice of 1 lime

1 teaspoon Maldon sea salt

1 jalapeño, seeded and minced (optional; leave on the side if serving kids)

½ cup fresh chopped cilantro

FOR SERVING

4 to 6 cups of your favorite greens

FOR THE FISH Place the fish in a glass baking dish. In a small bowl, combine the shallot, garlic, lemon juice, olive oil, and salt. Pour the mixture over the fish, cover with foil, and let the fish marinate for 1 hour in the refrigerator.

Preheat the oven to 400°F.

Remove foil, transfer the fish to the oven, and roast for 10 to 15 minutes. (You can also grill the fish on an outdoor grill.)

FOR THE SLAW While the fish is cooking, in a big bowl, toss together the red and napa cabbages, carrots, onion, cilantro, lemon juice, sea salt, and jalepeño (if using).

FOR THE DRESSING In a small bowl, mix the kefir, lime juice, sea salt, jalapeño (if using), and cilantro. Add the dressing to the slaw and toss.

TO PLATE Divide the fresh greens among four to six plates and top with the slaw and fish.

Young Lettuce Salad with Beet, Cacao Nibs, and Herbed Kefir Dressing

Cacao adds a rich element of surprise to this composed salad. You get sweetness, earthiness, and bitterness from the greens and the beets, then the probiotic tang of the herbed kefir dressing. The cacao adds a beautiful crunch before it literally melts in your mouth. Because cacao is high in astringent substances called tannins, I like to drizzle some extra virgin olive oil over this salad; the fat in the oil softens those tannins so the nibs taste less bitter, more bittersweet. (This same mellowing out effect is one reason red wine, also high in tannins, pairs so brilliantly with cheese.) The result: a sleek, sexy, uniquely delicious salad that harnesses loads of nutrition.

SERVES 4

2 pounds small red beets

½ cup extra virgin olive oil

Maldon sea salt and freshly cracked black pepper

Juice of ½ lemon, or more to taste

2 heads baby lettuce, torn or roughly chopped

1 cup Basic Herbed Kefir Dressing (page 46)

¼ cup cacao nibs

High-quality extra virgin olive oil, for drizzling

Preheat the oven to 375°F.

Slice the tops off of the beets and wash the bulbs thoroughly. Toss the beets with the olive oil to coat, then sprinkle with a pinch each of sea salt and pepper. Arrange in a shallow roasting pan, add about ¼ inch water to the pan, and cover with foil. Roast until a small knife easily pierces the beets, 45 to 60 minutes. When cool enough to handle, use your hands and a towel to slide the peels off under cold running water. Cut the beets into wedges and toss them with the lemon juice and a pinch of sea salt. Set aside.

Toss the lettuces with the dressing and a pinch of sea salt, seasoning with more lemon juice if needed. Divide the salad among four plates, topping with the beets and cacao nibs. Drizzle with high-quality olive oil before serving.

CHEF'S TIPS

Never throw out beet greens; they're delicious sautéed with olive oil, salt, and pepper.

Fingertips stained fuchsia? The same pigments that lend beets their awesome nutritional prowess will turn your hands pink in the blink of an eye. Not to worry: Just sprinkle a little baking soda over the stains and gently massage it in to remove the stains.

Brussels Sprouts and Apple Salad

Brussels sprouts are one of those foods that tend to divide people; you either really like them or really don't. Personally, I am wholeheartedly Team Brussels Sprouts, and I'm willing to bet that after you try this salad, you will be, too.

These little green orbs look like cute mini cabbages (in fact, they're in the same family), but they have a milder flavor. Deep within those tightly packed leaves hides an almost endless store of nutrients: Vitamins C and K, potassium, and folate, a critical nutrient for women of childbearing age. Plus, Brussels sprouts are extremely filling while also being low in calories—an entire cup has just 75 calories—so they're a smart choice for maintaining a healthy weight.

Sweet, crisp Fuji apples gives these Brussels an autumnal twist. (Keep the skin on those Fujis for extra fiber.) The sweetness of the apples complements the slight bitterness of the radicchio or endive; the end result is Fall on a Plate

SERVES 4

DRESSING

1 cup organic plain whole-milk kefir

¼ cup apple cider vinegar

½ cup roasted pumpkin seed oil

Maldon sea salt

PUMPKIN SEEDS

¼ cup pumpkin seeds

Leaves from 1 sprig fresh rosemary, chopped

FOR SERVING

1 pound trimmed Brussels sprouts, pulled apart into leaves

1 Fuji apple, unpeeled and sliced on a mandoline

3 medium radishes, sliced

1 head Treviso radicchio or Belgian endive, shaved on a mandoline

½ cup finely grated fresh horseradish

FOR THE DRESSING In a bowl, whisk together the kefir, vinegar, pumpkin oil, and a pinch of sea salt. Set aside.

FOR THE PUMPKIN SEEDS Preheat the oven to 325°F.

Spread the pumpkin seeds and chopped rosemary across a baking sheet and toast them in the oven for 8 minutes. (Be sure to set a timer, as these ingredients burn very easily.)

TO PLATE In a bowl, combine the Brussels sprouts, apple, radishes, radicchio, and horseradish. Add a pinch of sea salt and half of the dressing and gently toss. Taste and adjust the seasoning as needed. Add more dressing if needed. Evenly divide salad among four plates and top with the pumpkin seeds and rosemary.

Rye Berry Salad with Herbed Kefir Dressing

For centuries, rye has starred in Northern European cuisine; it's a staple of the New Nordic Diet, a nutrition lifestyle plan created in 2004 by a group of chefs, nutritionists, and other health experts in response to rising obesity rates in Sweden, Finland, Norway, Denmark, and Iceland. This nutrition lifestyle includes plenty of carrots, beets, and other root vegetables, fatty fish like salmon and herring, and small amounts of high-quality, grass-fed meats like bison and even elk . . . and rye bread is relied on for its high fiber content—two to three times the fiber of refined wheat bread.

Rye bread is made with chewy, nutty rye berries, which serve as the base of this deeply satisfying salad and give it its staying power. Just a small portion will keep you full for hours; chewing and digesting all that fiber (6 grams per ¼ cup dry berries) takes time and energy, meaning you'll stay fuller, longer. Rye berries are also very high in manganese, which aids in healthy brain, bone, and connective tissue functioning. These hearty grains keep their shape well, so this salad will keep well for up to a week in your refrigerator.

SERVES 4

2 cups rye berries

6 cups water

Kosher salt, for cooking the rye berries

4 tablespoons extra virgin olive oil

6 rainbow baby carrots, unpeeled and diced

Maldon sea salt

1 tablespoon lemon juice

½ cup Fried Onions (page 164)

1 tablespoon chopped fresh flat-leaf parsley

1 cup Basic Herbed Kefir Dressing (page 46)

¼ cup sherry vinegar

Freshly cracked black pepper

3 tablespoons grated fresh horseradish

In a saucepan, combine the rye berries and water and salt the water. Bring it to a boil, then reduce to a simmer and cook until al dente, 45 to 60 minutes. Drain, then spread the berries out on a large rimmed baking sheet to cool.

In a sauté pan, heat 2 tablespoons of the olive oil over medium heat. Add the carrots and sauté until golden brown and/or fork-tender, about 7 minutes. Remove them from the heat, season with a pinch of sea salt and the lemon juice, and let cool slightly.

In a medium bowl, combine the rye berries, carrots, fried onions, and parsley. Drizzle with the kefir dressing, vinegar, and the remaining 2 tablespoons olive oil and toss to combine. Season with a pinch each of sea salt and pepper, top with the horseradish and serve.

CHEF'S TIP Leave your carrots unpeeled. As long as they're washed well, the peels are perfectly safe to eat. You'll save time, plus you'll eke every last drop of nutrition out of them.

Frisée Salad with Avocado Kefir Goddess Dressing

Frisée (pronounced "free-ZAY") is a crunchy, lacy lettuce with a mildly bitter edge that can stand up to strong flavors. Here, I've paired it with quick pickled onions and spicy breakfast radishes. The endive's curly, or "frizzy," leaves are perfect for catching the grassy goddess dressing, which gets its creaminess from kefir instead of mayonnaise, buttermilk, or sour cream.

SERVES 4

ONIONS

1 small red onion, thinly sliced

Juice of 1 lime

Pinch of kosher salt

DRESSING

½ cup organic plain whole-milk kefir

1 medium avocado, pitted and peeled

2 tablespoons lemon juice

1 bunch fresh chives

1 bunch fresh parsley (1 inch of stems trimmed and discarded)

½ cup loosely packed fresh tarragon leaves

1 clove garlic, peeled

Maldon sea salt

¼ cup extra virgin olive oil

FOR SERVING

1 head frisée, roughly chopped

1 head green or red leaf lettuce, torn into small pieces

1 cup breakfast radishes, quartered

FOR THE ONIONS Soak the red onion in the lime juice and kosher salt for 30 minutes. Drain and discard the liquid.

FOR THE DRESSING In a blender, combine the kefir, half of the avocado, the lemon juice, chives, parsley, tarragon, garlic, and a pinch of sea salt. Puree and, with the blender running, drizzle the olive oil in slowly, until the dressing is smooth and has a beautiful dark avocado green color. Taste and add more sea salt if needed.

TO PLATE In a large bowl, combine the frisée, lettuce, drained onions, and radishes. Add the goddess dressing to the sides of the bowl (see Chef's tip) and mix well. Season with more sea salt if needed. Transfer the salad to a large platter and garnish with the remaining avocado, sliced.

CHEF'S TIP When dressing salads, always pour the dressing in along the *sides* of the bowl, then gently mix the salad against the sides. This avoids the thick clump of wet leaves that can result if you add all of the dressing to the middle of the salad.

Beet and Fig Salad with Candied Pecans

I dig figs, plain and simple—I love how when you bite through their velvety skin, you get that surprise mixture of jam with a hint of crunch from the teeny seeds. Dried figs manage to somehow feel rustic yet decadent at the same time; fresh ones, like this salad's deep purple Black Mission figs, with their luscious pink interior, are flat-out sexy.

Many of the ingredients in this standout, multidimensional dish—figs, beets, arugula— hit their peak in the fall, making an autumn farmers' market your perfect one-stop shop. The figs' earthiness and sweetness work particularly well with the tang of the labneh and the spiciness of the arugula; the pecans and honey click well, too. Pair this salad with a glass of Pinot Noir for a taste of Napa Valley spa cuisine right in your own home.

SERVES 4

CANDIED PECANS

½ cup pecans

2 tablespoons honey

BEETS

2 pounds small red beets

1½ cups extra virgin olive oil

Maldon sea salt and freshly cracked black pepper

Juice of 1 lemon

FOR SERVING

4 to 6 cups arugula

1 pint fresh Black Mission figs

½ cup Kefir Labneh (page 43)

CONCENTRATED GOODNESS

Soft, chewy figs are heavy with antioxidants, vitamins, and fiber. When shopping for the Black Mission figs in this recipe, look for deep brown or blackish-purple figs that are firm but not hard.

FOR THE CANDIED PECANS Preheat the oven to 335°F.

In a small ovenproof sauté pan, combine the pecans and honey and place in the oven. After 5 minutes, stir the pan to evenly coat the pecans with the now-melted honey. After another 5 minutes, stir again. After a final 5 minutes, remove the pan from the oven and empty the nuts out onto parchment paper, making sure to separate each nut so they don't stick together once cool.

FOR THE BEETS Preheat the oven to 375°F.

Slice the tops off the beets and wash the beets thoroughly. Toss the beets with enough olive oil to coat (about ½ cup) and a pinch each of sea salt and pepper. Place in a shallow roasting pan, add about ¼ inch water to the pan, and cover with foil. Roast until a small knife easily pierces a beet, 45 to 60 minutes. When cool enough to handle, use your hands and a towel to slide the peels off under cold running water. Cut the beets into wedges and toss them with half of the lemon juice, a pinch of sea salt, and ½ cup olive oil. Set aside.

TO PLATE In a bowl, toss the arugula with a pinch of sea salt and the remaining lemon juice and olive oil and divide among four plates. Add the figs to the bowl that had the arugula and toss with whatever dressing is still in the bowl (give them a good stir to coat). Arrange the figs atop the arugula. Add the beets and pecans to the plates in the same manner and garnish with small dollops of labneh.

HINT, HINT.

This is a good salad to make if you're planning a romantic date night: Beets are rich in compounds that help dilate blood vessels and boost blood flow to many parts of the body, including the sexual organs.

Hummus

Like most things in the Middle East, the origins of this ancient tangy dip have been disputed for centuries. Hummus is not just the food of a country, it's the food of an entire region—Lebanon, Turkey, Israel, Palestine, Greece, Syria, Egypt, and even India, just to name a few, all pay homage to this dish or a variation of it, thereby creating a heated debate. As a matter of fact, while some wars are said to have been started over love, others have been started over hummus. Yes, highly contentious hummus wars have actually occurred. Plato and Socrates helped elevate its status when they referenced it in their writings. Chickpeas, the star of this dish, are one of the oldest crops in the world. It is said that their origins date back to utopia and the Gardens of Babylon, where rivers ran deep and the hummus, legend says, ran smooth and creamy.

Fiber-rich chickpeas drowning in a pool of olive oil and sesame tahini—not a bad way to go. This dip is pure Mediterranean goodness, through and through.

SERVES 4

2 cups cooked chickpeas (reserve the cooking liquid) or one 16-ounce can chickpeas, drained and liquid reserved

¼ cup organic plain whole-milk kefir

1 head Roasted Garlic (page 45)

Juice of 1 lemon

Pinch of Maldon sea salt

½ cup tahini (sesame paste)

¼ cup extra virgin olive oil

High-quality extra virgin olive oil, for drizzling

½ teaspoon smoked paprika

Pinch of ground cumin

1 tablespoon chopped fresh flat-leaf parsley

A platter of your favorite crudités, plus corn chips and pita bread

A DUNK OF HUMMUS A DAY KEEPS THE DOCTOR AWAY

Hummus is a no-brainer way to achieve the recommended 1½ cups of legumes per week: Just ¼ cup a day nets you 2 cups of legumes per week, plus 14 grams of plant protein. Hummus-lovers consume more fiber, poly-unsaturated fatty acids, magnesium, potassium, iron, folate, and vitamins A, C, and E compared with non-*hummusseurs*, per a 2016 study. That same study found that eating hummus may even prevent or offset the development of multiple chronic diseases, including heart disease and type 2 diabetes. Hummus also contains four to five times more fat than plain chickpeas, and those good fats are thought to help stabilize blood sugar levels and keep you fuller, longer.

In a food processor, combine the chickpeas and grind as fine as possible. Transfer the bowl of the food processor to the refrigerator and chill the ground chickpeas for about 15 minutes.

Add the kefir, roasted garlic, lemon juice, salt, tahini, and ¼ cup olive oil to the food processor and blend until you reach your desired texture—the finer the puree, the better. If the hummus is too thick, add some of the reserved chickpea cooking liquid or canned chickpea liquid. It should be thinner than the actual desired texture, because it will thicken back up. Serve in a bowl with a good drizzling of olive oil, and sprinkle with the paprika, cumin, and chopped parsley. I love dipping blue corn chips into hummus for an elevated "chips and dip," but pita and veggies work well, too.

Variations

ZA'ATAR For more complex flavor (sumac, thyme, sesame), dust some of this quintessential Middle Eastern spice on top of your hummus before serving. Warning: Habit-forming. (Za'atar also tastes great mixed with olive oil and sopped up with bread, or dusted on labneh.)

SWEET PEA Replace chickpeas with an equal amount of cooked sweet, green peas.

TOPPINGS BAR Serve hummus with sides of roasted mushrooms, cubed roasted squash, sliced Greek olives and feta cheese, sliced hard-boiled eggs, crunchy kale chips, whole chickpeas, and extra tahini.

CHEF'S TIP Feel free to use canned chickpeas here if you don't have time to soak and prep dry beans; canned beans work best in purees or other recipes where appearance and firmness don't matter.

Eggplant Baba Ghanoush

I had the special honor of spending International Holocaust Remembrance Day in Jerusalem, at the home of celebrated Israeli Chef Shmil Holland. The evening of my visit happened to be Shabbat, the Jewish day of rest that begins Friday at nightfall and ends Saturday evening. Chef Shmil's table was loaded with drool-worthy foods: Traditional Shabbat fare, like home-made yeasty, eggy, braided challah, plus a slew of local Mediterranean favorites: hummus, falafel, and baba ghanoush, a smoky eggplant dip. Also on the table were candlesticks and a small, tulip-shaped silver Kiddush cup. Kiddush means sanctification in Hebrew, and on Shabbat eve (as well as at weddings, Bar and Bat Mitzvahs, baby namings, and other celebrations), it is filled with wine and a special prayer is recited over it.

Chef shared the history of this particular Kiddush cup with the other guests and me: It belonged to his grandfather's grandfather. It was the only personal item that his family was able to bring with them when they were deported to one of the concentration camps. Despite the pain and devastation of their situation, family members passed the empty cup around every Friday night. They barely had food or water, let alone wine. But they per-sisted. This was their form of spiritual resistance. Chef let me sip wine from the cup. I had instant shivers, holding such an extraordinary ancient artifact—one that holds the soul of six million Jews.

After we all sipped and said a prayer for those who perished, we moved on to the celebratory part of Shabbat: the food. One dish that stood out in particular was the baba ghanoush. Chef Shmil had grilled the eggplant over an open flame, infus-ing the dish with a rich, fire-roasted flavor. I decided to try replicating this meze platter staple at home, using my trusty oven to achieve that won-derful smokiness. The brightness from the lemon really wakes up your palate. Every time I make this, I think of that special Shabbat in Jerusalem.

With Chef Shmil Holland and his grandfather's grandfather's Kiddush cup at his home in Jerusalem on Holocaust Remembrance Day.

1 large eggplant

¼ cup extra virgin olive oil

¼ cup tahini (sesame paste)

1 head Roasted Garlic (page 45)

Juice of 1 lemon

¼ cup organic plain whole-milk kefir, plus more if needed

Maldon sea salt

Dusting of smoked paprika

Dusting of ground cumin

1 teaspoon chopped fresh oregano

A platter of your favorite crudités, plus pita bread or pita chips

Preheat the oven to 475°F. Line a baking sheet with foil.

Rub the outside of the eggplant with the olive oil and place it on the baking sheet. Roast the eggplant until the skin has charred and the interior is tender, 45 to 60 minutes. When cool enough to handle, peel and seed the eggplant, then roughly chop the flesh and transfer it to a food processor.

Add the tahini, roasted garlic, lemon juice, kefir, and 1 to 2 pinches of sea salt. Process the mixture to a coarse paste, adding a bit more kefir as needed to allow the mixture to blend. Add more salt to taste, pour into a serving bowl, dust with paprika and cumin and top with oregano. Serve with crudités and pita bread or chips. (Baba ghanoush also makes a nice sandwich spread.)

Olivier Potato Salad

Olivier potato salad is one of the foods my family has always eaten when welcoming the New Year, or at any family gathering, really; it's basically sacrilegious to not offer it. For non-Russians, the classic Olivier formula can seem a bit . . . interesting: Gobs of mayonnaise, chopped bologna, gherkin pickles, and peas. Still, it was a customary dish, and by the time I was twelve years old, I knew the recipe inside and out, and was tasked with assembling an enormous bowl of it before guests arrived. I'd snack on bologna bits as I prepped the ingredients, like most kids sneak chocolate chips when baking cookies. Once all of our recently immigrated friends arrived at our townhouse, I'd set out the massive platter of Olivier salad, along with some of my mom's Russian salad, smoked trout, pickled vegetables, sliced cheese, and meats, and we'd put away bowl after bowl.

The updated version you see here features mortadella, a cured Italian meat, instead of bologna, and replaces most of the heavy mayonnaise with kefir.

SERVES 2

3 small red potatoes, cut into ½-inch cubes

Kosher salt, for the cooking water

3 large brown eggs, hard-boiled, peeled, and diced, plus 1 extra hard-boiled egg, peeled and cut into wedges, for garnish

⅕ pound organic plain whole-milk kefir

2 tablespoons mayonnaise

1 tablespoon extra virgin olive oil

1 tablespoon mustard

Maldon sea salt

1 red carrot, unpeeled and grated

⅕ medium red onion, chopped

1 green onion, chopped

3 medium gherkin pickles, chopped

1 cup fresh peas

1 pound mortadella, diced

Freshly cracked black pepper

Chopped dill, for garnish

In a large pot of lightly salted water that is almost (but not yet) boiling, cook the potatoes for 20 minutes. Drain and let cool.

In a bowl, combine the chopped egg, kefir, mayonnaise, olive oil, and mustard with a pinch of Maldon salt. Add the cooled potatoes, carrot, red onion, green onion, and pickles.

Bring a small pot of salted water to a boil. Submerge the peas in the boiling water for 1 minute and taste; they are best crunchy. (If still too hard, keep submerged an extra 30 seconds.) Drain and add the peas to the potato mix, along with the mortadella and stir gently to combine. Season with sea salt and pepper, top with the chopped dill, and serve. Garnish with egg wedges.

PROBIOTIC POWER

The chilled potatoes in this salad contain a type of carbohydrate called resistant starch. Our bodies cannot digest resistant starch (it's resistant to digestion, hence the name), so it sails through the stomach to the gut, where it acts like a prebiotic, fueling your healthy bacteria as they strive to keep your system in balance. That means the potatoes in this dish act as fuel for the kefir. The trick to making the resistant starch in potatoes work for you: Eat them cold. The starch is created as the cooked potato cools; reheating the potato breaks down the starch. Get more cold potato goodness with some Chilled Okroshka (page 176), Ludmila's Borscht (page 168), Potato Leek Vichyssoise—so long as you eat it cold (page 187), and Sweet Potato Pie (page 306).

Kidney Bean and Veggie Salad

Here's your new go-to recipe for when you need something easy, healthy, and tasty to bring to a party or picnic (it also makes for an easy lunch to eat at your desk if you can't escape from work). Kidney beans are rich in hunger-busting protein and fiber—almost 14 grams per cup of each—and they're high in antioxidant zinc and manganese, plus phosphorus, a multitalented mineral that helps filter waste from the kidneys, reduces postworkout muscle soreness, and is necessary for the maintenance, growth, and repair of basically every tissue and cell in the body. With rainbow carrots, golden beets, bright radishes, and green herbs, the finished dish looks like edible confetti. Simple and delicious.

SERVES 4

BEETS

1 pound golden beets

¼ cup plus 2 tablespoons extra virgin olive oil

Maldon sea salt and freshly cracked black pepper

SHALLOTS

½ cup sliced shallots

2 tablespoons sherry vinegar

FOR SERVING

1 cup dried kidney beans, cooked, or one 16-ounce can kidney beans, drained

½ cup sliced radishes

½ cup diced unpeeled rainbow carrots

1 cup Basic Herbed Kefir Dressing (page 46)

½ cup cilantro leaves

½ cup mint leaves

DID YOU KNOW . . .

This dish was inspired by *lobio,* a kidney bean stew enjoyed day and night in the Caucasus mountains, the same region where kefir was born.

FOR THE BEETS Preheat the oven to 375°F.

Slice the tops off of the beets and wash the beets thoroughly. Toss the beets with enough olive oil to coat (about ¼ cup), season with sea salt and pepper, and place in a shallow roasting pan. Add about ¼ inch water to the pan, cover with foil, and roast until a small knife easily pierces a beet, 45 to 60 minutes. When cool enough to handle, use your hands and a towel to slide the peels off under cold running water. Quarter a few beets, enough to yield ½ cup, and set aside. (Save the remaining beets for another recipe.)

FOR THE SHALLOTS While the beets are roasting, soak the sliced shallots in the sherry vinegar for 30 minutes, then drain and discard the liquid.

TO PLATE In a bowl, combine the kidney beans, radishes, carrots, beets, and shallots. Add 1 tablespoon Maldon salt, the kefir dressing, and the remaining 2 tablespoons olive oil, mixing until thoroughly incorporated. Place the entire mixture on a serving dish and garnish with the cilantro and mint leaves.

Kefir Labneh French Onion Dip

This dip will change your life, it's that good. I dare you not to lick the spoon.

SERVES 4

¼ cup brandy

½ cup beef broth

1 tablespoon minced shallots

½ teaspoon freshly cracked black pepper

Kefir Labneh (page 43)

¼ cup Fried Onions (page 164), plus a small handful for garnish

1 teaspoon Maldon sea salt

Salt and vinegar potato chips (or your favorite potato chips), for dipping

In a saucepan, combine the brandy, beef broth, shallots, and black pepper. Reduce over low heat until syrupy, about 10 minutes. Set aside to cool.

In a bowl, combine the labneh, the ¼ cup fried onions, sea salt, and the cooled syrup. Mix until smooth and incorporated (there should be no white areas). Transfer the dip to a bowl and garnish with the extra fried onions. Serve with chips.

Fried Onions

These are reminiscent of the canned fried onions you've likely had at Thanksgiving, only healthier and far more delicious.

MAKES ½ CUP

1 medium yellow onion

1 cup Kefir Ghee (page 41)

Pinch of Maldon sea salt

Slice the onion with the grain (pole to pole, not through the equator). In a saucepan, heat the ghee over medium heat. Add the onions and cook, stirring until the onions are evenly browned and almost crunchy, 15 to 20 minutes. Place them in a mason jar, seasoning with a pinch of sea salt.

CHEF'S TIP Don't be tempted to buy that grapefruit-size onion you spot at the market; it's full of water, diluting the natural sugars inside. Always select small-to-medium onions.

Tzatziki

The Greeks have really taken full ownership and run with this creamy addictive mezze dip, and the sultans of the Ottoman Empire would like to claim victory as the original architects of stirring it into existence in the fifteenth and sixteenth centuries, but some believe that it actually originated in India as a version of "raita" when Indian chefs, responsible for cooking the meals of the ruling Persian Muslim elite, offered a cool creamy yogurt dip to counter the heat of strong Indian spices people were unaccustomed to enjoying. Eventually, this condiment traveled along Ottoman trade routes, establishing itself as a staple in Byzantine cuisine. Crunchy, fresh cucumbers and the mouthwatering flavors of minced garlic, freshly cut mint, and dill bring this sauce to life and make it fit for a king, queen, sultan, or princess. Still, I can't help but feel transported to the land of Greek isles, where vibrant bougainvillea vines climb whitewashed buildings, domed roofs are as blue as the seas, and sunsets blaze the sky in pink, purple, orange, and red hues. Use this tzatziki on grilled meats and chicken, or as a dip for your favorite crunchy vegetables or pita chips.

SERVES 4

1 cucumber

Maldon sea salt

1 cup organic plain whole-milk kefir

1 tablespoon Kefir Labneh (page 43)

¼ cup combined chopped fresh dill and mint

2 cloves of garlic, peeled and minced

¼ cup extra virgin olive oil

Peel the cucumber, leaving stripes of green skin intact for color. (The end result will be a "striped" cucumber.) Halve the cucumber lengthwise, scoop out the seeds with a spoon, and grate the flesh using a fine cheese grater.

Place the cucumber in a bowl with a pinch of sea salt and allow to sit for 1 hour, then pour the mixture into a sieve to drain it of any excess juices. (Don't skip this step; it's crucial for avoiding a watery tzatziki.) Combine the drained, chopped cucumber with the kefir labneh, chopped dill and mint, garlic, olive oil, and ½ teaspoon salt. Mix and taste, adding more salt if needed. Refrigerate for at least 1 hour to let the flavors meld—but it tastes even better when refrigerated overnight.

White Bean Puree

This dip has the smooth, creamy mouthfeel of hummus, but stars cannellini beans, also known as white kidney beans. Try it on bruschetta or crostini, topped with sun-dried tomatoes.

SERVES 4

1 cup dried cannellini beans, cooked (reserve the cooking liquid) or one 16-ounce can cannellini beans, drained and liquid reserved

¾ cup organic plain whole-milk kefir

1 head Roasted Garlic (page 45)

¼ cup lemon juice

1 teaspoon chopped fresh thyme

Pinch of Maldon sea salt

¼ cup extra virgin olive oil

Good-quality extra virgin olive oil, for drizzling

In a food processor, grind the beans well; the texture should be somewhere between fine and chunky. Transfer the bowl of the food processor to the refrigerator and chill the ground beans for about 15 minutes.

Add the kefir, roasted garlic, lemon juice, thyme, salt, and olive oil to the food processor and blend until you reach your desired texture—the finer the puree, the better. If the puree is too thick, add some of the reserved cooking liquid or canned bean liquid. It should be thinner than the actual desired texture, because it will thicken back up. Serve with an extra drizzle of olive oil.

PROBIOTIC POWER

With two prebiotic ingredients—garlic and cannellini beans—along with the probiotics in the kefir, this is one seriously gut-friendly dip.

SOUPS

Lunch or dinner isn't complete for me without soup. Soup is the ultimate chameleon—it tastes great hot or cold; pureed or chunky. It's light enough for an appetizer but satisfying enough to stand alone as a meal.

Personally, I love how nourishing and healing soups feel; warming in the winter, detoxifying when I'm under the weather. There's something about sipping soup that's just good for the soul.

Kefir lends a bright acidity and mouth-watering quality to vegetable-based soups like Ludmila's Borscht (page 168) and the Butternut Squash and Pumpkin Soup (page 171); a cooling effect to Chilled Cucumber-Avocado Soup (page 175), and good-for-you creaminess to Potato Leek Vichyssoise (page 187). Some of these soups can be made with ingredients from your backyard garden and will be ready in 20 minutes; others will take more time but are worth the effort.

Ludmila's Borscht

Growing up, my brother and I would head home from school, fling our backpacks off, and head straight for the kitchen, where two bowls of our mom's borscht would be waiting for us in the refrigerator. The color was to die for—a shocking, vibrant magenta that seemed to cool you off just by looking at it. (It wasn't until I was an adult that I learned my mom's trick: A squeeze of lemon, added after the beets had boiled, provided just enough acid to make the color come alive.)

Every Russian or Ukrainian seems to have their own personalized version of this classic beet soup: Some throw in potatoes, carrots, and eggs, resulting in a thick, almost gazpacho-like texture; others stick with just a few simple ingredients, resulting in a soup so light you can drink it from a glass. But we all seem to agree on a few key features: The rich earthiness of beets, the grassiness of dill, and the creaminess of cold dairy. In my family, we've always used kefir in place of sour cream; its palate-pleasing tang perfectly balances the beets' natural sweetness. I suggest letting your family or guests pour the kefir in on their own—they'll love the experience of watching the deep red soup turn raspberry pink, like dark roasted coffee clouding up with cream. Get ready to enjoy an uplifting taste of the Old World.

SERVES 6

12 cups water

4 red beets, ends trimmed, peeled

1 large cucumber, peeled and diced

Juice of ½ lemon

2 large brown eggs, hard-boiled, peeled, and diced, plus 1 extra hard-boiled egg cut into wedges, for garnish

6 tablespoons chopped fresh dill

3 cups organic plain whole-milk kefir

Black bread, for dunking

In a saucepan, bring the water to a boil while you peel and trim the beets and peel and dice the cucumber. Once the water has reached a rolling boil, add the beets and cook for 30 minutes. Remove the pot from the heat and add the lemon juice. Once the pot has cooled off, transfer it to the refrigerator for 4 hours or overnight.

Remove the beets, dice them, and return them to the soup. Divide the soup among six bowls and add equal amounts of diced cucumber and chopped egg to each serving, topping each with 1 tablespoon chopped dill. Everyone then gets a ½ cup kefir to swirl in prior to enjoying. Garnish with egg wedges and serve with a slice of black bread for dunking. If you can force yourself to wait, this soup is even better the next day.

THE BENEFITS OF BEETS

Borscht might not be the sexiest sounding name, but it's showing up on the menu at all the hottest restaurants. In addition to their stunning color, beets are wildly nutritious, packed with iron, potassium, magnesium, folate, vitamins A, B6, and C, and more. Pigments called betalains, responsible for this root vegetable's brilliant, saturated hue, are revered by scientists for their potent anti-inflammatory properties, thought to protect arteries from damage, reduce the risk of heart disease and other chronic diseases, and more.

With my brother Ed.

Butternut Squash and Pumpkin Soup

Growing up, our family Thanksgivings didn't feature green bean casserole, pumpkin pie, or other typical fare; it was just Russian food, plus a turkey. As I entered my twenties, got my own apartment, and assumed the role of hostess, I began adding in little dashes of American Turkey Day cuisine. This soup has always been one of my favorites.

Russians aren't used to pumpkin soup, so I would swirl some kefir in tableside. That little, opaque white cloud in the middle of everyone's bowl helped my guests feel at home. It's a ritual that stuck—to this day, everyone loves when I do it.

SERVES 4 TO 6

1 small butternut squash, peeled, seeded, and cut into 1-inch cubes

4 tablespoons extra virgin olive oil

1 teaspoon kosher salt

2 cloves garlic, chopped

1 tablespoon minced fresh ginger

1 teaspoon chopped fresh rosemary

1 medium yellow onion, diced

2 tablespoons tomato paste

One 29-ounce can pure pumpkin puree

2 quarts cold water

¼ teaspoon freshly grated nutmeg, plus more for garnish

¼ teaspoon ground star anise

¼ teaspoon ground cloves

Maldon sea salt

1 teaspoon sherry vinegar

4 to 6 tablespoons Kefir Labneh (page 43)

¼ cup organic plain whole-milk kefir

Preheat the oven to 450°F.

Toss the squash with 2 tablespoons of the olive oil and spread them out on a baking sheet. Roast for 7 minutes, rotate the sheet front to back, sprinkle the kosher salt over the squash and roast for an additional 7 minutes

In a large pot, heat the remaining 2 tablespoons olive oil over medium-high heat. Add the garlic, ginger, and rosemary and cook until translucent, 3 to 5 minutes. Add the onions and cook until translucent, being careful to stir so as to not add any color. Stir in the tomato paste and cook until slightly darker, 3 to 5 minutes. Add the pumpkin, cold water, nutmeg, star anise, cloves, and a generous pinch of Maldon salt. Bring to a boil, then reduce to a simmer, partially cover the pot, and let simmer for 45 minutes to 1 hour, stirring every 10 minutes or so.

Remove the pot from the heat and let the soup cool slightly. Add it in batches to a blender with the sherry vinegar, pureeing until smooth. Divide among bowls and serve with a dollop (about 1 tablespoon) of the labneh and garnish with a little freshly grated nutmeg. Drizzle with the kefir.

STEP-SAVER Plain kefir works well in lieu of the labneh.

TIP This soup freezes well, so feel free to double the recipe and save half for the future. When reheating, place it in the fridge overnight, then gently reheat on the stovetop.

Ninety-five percent of all pumpkins in the United States are grown in Illinois. We always head down to the farm to pick our own for the fall season.

Chilled Cucumber-Avocado Soup

I love whipping up this refreshing, no-oven-necessary soup on a hot Chicago summer day. It's tart and refreshing, and the diced cucumbers on top add just the right amount of texture. Chances are you already have the ingredients in your kitchen as we speak, so what are you waiting for?

SERVES 4

1 cup organic plain whole-milk kefir

2 medium avocados, pitted and peeled, plus a few extra slices for garnish

3 medium Persian (mini) cucumbers (I use these because I like to leave the skin on. If you can't find Persian cucumbers, use any seedless variety.)

2 cups water

2 tablespoons champagne vinegar

½ cup fresh mint leaves, plus extra for garnish

1 teaspoon Maldon sea salt

2 tablespoons extra virgin olive oil

Diced cucumber, for garnish

In a blender, combine the kefir, avocados, cucumbers, water, vinegar, mint, and salt and puree until smooth, drizzling in the olive oil. Refrigerate the soup until chilled, a few hours. Divide among four bowls, topping each with mint leaves, sliced avocado, and diced cucumber.

Chilled Okroshka

My mother has a thing for beautiful shoes—her closet is filled with sleek black heels, sexy gladiator sandals, to-die-for boots. But it wasn't always this way. According to my mom:

When I was a child living in Ukraine, I used to spend the summer running around outside, playing with friends, until Mama called me home for dinner. My favorite was *okroshka*, a cold cucumber and potato soup. One summer, when I was eight years old, my older sister, Tamara, bought me a pair of black patent leather shoes. She was twenty-four and had to scrape together the money for these shoes; she wanted me to wear them for my first day of school, with my new hair ribbons. These shoes were my only pair at the time.

So, it was the summer and I wanted to visit a river in the forest near our house. Across the river there was a little bridge. I sat down on the bridge and was dangling my feet over the water when one shoe fell off. The current swept it away. I was terrified of what would happen to me, but it was getting dark and I knew I had to return home for dinner. My mother saw that I only had one shoe and I got a spanking. Then she served me *okroshka*.

This savory Russian gazpacho has been passed down through my family for generations. A refreshing blend of cucumbers, red potatoes, and dill, floating in a creamy pool of plain kefir and chicken broth, the name okroshka comes from the diced (or crushed, as the word suggests) nature of its ingredients. With a vegetable-to-liquid ratio similar to that of cereal and milk, my mother's soup is filling enough to stand alone as a meal but won't weigh you down, even after two bowls; I can never stop at one.

My mother as a young girl playing near the forest by her home in Kharkiv.

Chilled
Okroshka

Olivier Potato Salad

Ludmila's
Borscht

SERVES 4

1 cup diced cucumbers

1 large potato, unpeeled, boiled, and diced

4 large brown eggs, hard-boiled, peeled, and chopped, plus 2 extra, halved

1 pound organic chicken, cooked and shredded

Maldon sea salt

4 cups organic plain whole-milk kefir

3 tablespoons fresh dill, chopped

2 cups chicken broth

3 tablespoons diced green onions (white and green parts)

Freshly cracked black pepper

In a large bowl, combine the cucumbers, potatoes, eggs, chicken, and a pinch of sea salt and toss to combine. Distribute the salad among four shallow bowls. In a separate bowl, combine the kefir, dill, and chicken broth and season with a pinch of sea salt. Pour the kefir mixture evenly over the vegetables in the bowls, remembering you are looking for a milk-to-cereal ratio. Top each serving with green onions. Season with salt and pepper.

NOTE *Okroshka* is basically Olivier Potato Salad (page 158) in soup form.

CHEF'S TIP For the perfect hard-boiled egg—firm whites, creamy yolks—try this hack: Bring a pot of water to a boil. Once it starts boiling, add 1 teaspoon baking soda, then gently drop in your raw eggs and set a timer for 8 minutes. After 8 minutes, remove the eggs from the hot water and run under cool water (or drop them in a bowl of cool water) to stop the cooking. (My Renegade Muffins, page 65, only call for a 5-minute egg because of the additional cooking time once they reach the oven.)

Turkey Chili, Two Ways

This one-pot crowd-pleaser belongs to the greatest papa ever, Jason, who makes this chili for our girls every fall. It's built on classic chili ingredients like kidney beans and crushed tomatoes, but he swaps out the meat for ground turkey. (That's only because we happen to prefer turkey chili over beef; feel free to substitute an equal amount of ground beef if that's your preference.)

Jason's chili can be prepared two ways: On the stovetop or, if you don't have the time to supervise a bubbling pot of chili, in a crockpot. I like to cook overnight in a crockpot, letting the flavors meld all day long and then serving it the following evening.

SERVES 8

1½ teaspoons extra virgin olive oil

1 pound ground turkey

1 tablespoon minced garlic

1 medium yellow onion, chopped

One 28-ounce can crushed tomatoes

2 cups water

One 16-ounce can kidney beans, drained

One 16-ounce can black beans, drained

One 16-ounce can corn kernels, drained

1 teaspoon chili powder

½ teaspoon smoked paprika

½ teaspoon ground coriander

½ teaspoon ground cumin

½ teaspoon dried oregano

½ teaspoon Maldon sea salt

½ teaspoon freshly cracked black pepper

1 cup organic plain whole-milk kefir or Kefir Labneh (page 43)

STOVETOP VERSION In a large pot, heat the oil over medium heat. Add the turkey to the pot and cook until evenly browned, 5 to 7 minutes. Stir in the garlic and onion and cook until tender, about 5 minutes. Pour in the canned tomatoes and cook down, about 5 minutes. Add the water, beans, corn, chili powder, paprika, coriander, cumin, oregano, salt, and pepper. Bring the mixture to a boil, then reduce the heat to low and simmer, uncovered, for 30 minutes. Serve the chili with the kefir on the side and swirl it in just before eating.

CROCKPOT VERSION Heat the oil in a crockpot set on high heat. Add the turkey to the crockpot and cook until evenly browned, 5 to 7 minutes. Stir in the garlic and onion, and cook until tender, about 5 minutes. Then add the remaining ingredients (except the kefir or labneh). Cover and cook on low for 7 to 8 hours.

CHEF'S TIP
This chili freezes well, so I suggest doubling the recipe and saving half for the future. When reheating, place it in the fridge overnight, then gently reheat on the stovetop.

PARTY TIP

People love it when you serve anything with a toppings bar. From Bloody Marys to ice cream sundaes, people go crazy when they see a tantalizing display of customizable ingredients all laid out and ready to be mixed and matched. For this chili, try bowls of shredded sharp cheddar cheese, sliced green onions, cubed avocado, extra kidney beans, corn niblets, elbow pasta, crunchy tortilla strips, and, in lieu of sour cream, plain whole-milk kefir.

Peasant Fava Bean Barley Stew

This traditional Colombian dish is ultra inviting on a chilly fall evening. Fava beans, also known as broad beans, are a bit off the beaten path but are definitely worth trying; they're firmer than lima beans, look a bit like edamame, and have a nice "green" sort of taste.

SERVES 4

¼ cup organic plain whole-milk kefir

1 tablespoon chopped fresh flat-leaf parsley

3 tablespoons extra virgin olive oil

2 cloves garlic, sliced

1 yellow onion, diced

2 medium carrots, unpeeled and diced

2 ribs celery, diced

6 cups vegetable broth

½ cup pearl barley, cooked

2 cups, fresh, peeled fava beans, cooked

1 tablespoon Maldon sea salt

In a small bowl, mix the kefir and parsley together. Set aside.

In a large soup pot, heat the olive oil over medium heat. Add the garlic and cook until lightly browned. Add the onion, carrots, and celery and cook until the carrots are tender. Add the broth and bring to a soft boil, then reduce to a simmer. Add the barley and simmer for 15 minutes, then add the fava beans and season with the salt. Divide among four bowls, topping each with a tablespoon of the kefir/parsley mixture.

During the Middle Ages, folklore says, Sicily was struggling with a terrible drought. All of the crops had dried up and food was scarce. People prayed to St. Joseph, beseeching him to make it rain . . . and it did. The one crop that came back to life was the fava bean. Every year, on March 19, the people of Sicily celebrate this miracle with the Feast of St. Joseph, and if you were to attend a local parade, you would likely be showered with colorful strings of beads along with dried fava beans.

Exotic Mushroom and Barley Soup

Growing up, mushroom-barley soup was a staple in our kitchen. My mom created her own step-saver, supplementing two tubes of Manischewitz Vegetable with Mushrooms soup mix with dried mushrooms from her deli. My modernized version starts from scratch and incorporates the musky, umami flavor of truffles. What began as a crush on truffles has, for me, evolved into a wild love affair; I'm a total sucker for their pungent, heady scent. That said, truffles can be crazy expensive. (In the foodie world, they're often called "underground diamonds.") Thankfully, Mother Nature has smiled down on us, as a little bit of truffle goes a long way; they actually taste best when used sparingly. In this dish, the bulk of the umami flavor comes from an assortment of mixed exotic mushrooms, and the hit of truffle oil (or fresh truffles, if you're lucky) at the end is just enough to satisfy your inner truffle fiend.

SERVES 4

¼ cup extra virgin olive oil

1 pound mixed exotic mushrooms (shiitakes, maitakes, morels), trimmed and sliced

2 cloves garlic, sliced

½ cup chopped leek (white and light green parts)

½ cup white wine

6 cups vegetable broth

½ cup pearl barley, cooked

1 tablespoon truffle salt

1 cup organic plain whole-milk kefir

¼ cup chopped fresh tarragon

Truffle oil *or* shaved fresh truffles, for garnish

In a large soup pot, heat the olive oil over medium heat. Add the mushrooms to the pot, evenly distributing them over the bottom of the pot. Let the mushrooms sit, without stirring, until browned, 7 to 10 minutes. Once the moisture has evaporated, give a quick stir, then add the garlic and the leek, cooking until slightly browned. Add the white wine and stir with a wooden spoon, scraping up any cooked bits off the bottom of the pot. Once the wine has been reduced by half, add the vegetable broth and bring to a slow boil. Reduce to a simmer, add the barley and truffle salt, and let simmer for 15 minutes. Remove the soup from the heat before stirring in the kefir and the tarragon, mixing well. Divide among four bowls, garnishing each with a drizzle of truffle oil *or* shaved truffle.

CHEF'S TIP Try not to stir your mushrooms too early; listen for the sizzling sound of moisture evaporating before stirring. If you jump the gun, you'll wind up with soggy, watery mushrooms instead of the caramelized gems you want.

Potato Leek Vichyssoise

This silky soup is delicious hot or chilled. Leeks are considered prebiotics, so they'll help power the probiotics in the whole-milk kefir, kefir butter, and kefir labneh. You can use an equal amount of steamed cauliflower in place of the potatoes for a light cauliflower chowder.

SERVES 4

2 tablespoons Cultured Kefir Butter (page 35)

1 leek, cleaned and chopped (white and light green parts)

2 cloves garlic, chopped

2 cups water

2 medium russet potatoes, peeled and diced

Maldon sea salt

2 cups organic plain whole-milk kefir

2 teaspoons fresh thyme leaves

Juice of 1 lemon

4 teaspoons Kefir Labneh (page 43)

Extra virgin olive oil, for drizzling

In a large soup pot, melt the kefir butter over low heat. Add the leek and garlic and cook, stirring frequently until translucent, about 10 minutes. Add the water, potatoes, and 1 teaspoon Maldon sea salt. Bring to a boil, then reduce the heat and cook, partially covered, for 1 hour 30 minutes. Remove the pot from the heat and allow the soup to cool slightly. Working in batches, puree the soup in a blender or food processor until you reach a smooth consistency. Stir in the kefir and 1 teaspoon of the thyme. Season to taste with salt and add the lemon juice and refrigerate until chilled. To serve, divide the soup among four bowls and top each with 1 teaspoon labneh, a drizzle of olive oil, and the remaining thyme.

Seamus Mullen's Carrot Soup with Kefir and Dill

RECIPE COURTESY OF SEAMUS MULLEN

"If you happened to catch me while competing on The Next Iron Chef *in 2009, you probably had no idea that, behind the scenes, in between racing across the kitchen and against the clock, I was in a wheelchair. Just two years earlier, I had been diagnosed with rheumatoid arthritis, an incurable autoimmune disease in which chronic inflammation causes joint pain, swelling, and immobility. For me, the pain was agonizing. Not too long after* Iron Chef *wrapped, I landed in the hospital, where doctors discovered almost forty blood clots scattered throughout my body. I almost didn't make it.*

"One day soon after that hospital stay, I caught a glimpse of myself in the mirror. I missed the athletic, energetic man I had once been—I had been a huge adrenaline junkie, big into adventure travel and mountain biking. I missed being able to use my most valuable kitchen tool—my hands—because of pain. So I decided to make some changes. Having grown up on an organic farm in Vermont, my mother and grandmother had taught me early on the power of locally grown, farm-to-table food, but I had strayed as I grew older, turning to salty, fatty, and sugary foods, along with, as I now like to call them, 'food-like items.' I began scouring books by respected nutritionists and physicians, learning that the system-wide inflammation responsible for my symptoms could be managed, and maybe even improved, with food. My diet transformed; I loaded up on whole, naturally anti-inflammatory foods like seasonal organic produce and wild seafood, as well as probiotic-rich fermented foods like kefir and kimchi. I said goodbye to alcohol, grain-fed meat, and any ingredients I couldn't pronounce. I also saw an acupuncturist, took probiotic supplements, and utilized other holistic therapies. Within one year, my pain was gone, I was off all of my medications, and my doctors could no longer detect any signs of rheumatoid arthritis in my blood. I've also lost fifty pounds and have become a competitive cyclist.

"Not surprisingly, Julie and I met at a wellness fest in Montauk a few summers ago.

"It didn't take long to realize that the two of us shared the belief that food has the power to heal, or poison, the body. We joined forces that day in Montauk, and we've been collaborating ever since, on everything from recipe development and blog posts to the dishes I conceptualized and cooked for a four-day Food Network & Cooking Channel NYC Wine & Food Festival: *a savory almond-based, gluten-free muffin using plain kefir and a rosemary, citrus, and garlic spread with farmer cheese.*

"For The Kefir Cookbook, I've created a carrot, kefir, and dill soup. Carrots are a great way of brightening up the winter doldrums; they're delicious and dense with nutrients. The fresh turmeric adds vibrancy, and the kefir offers creaminess, healthy fats, proteins, and probiotics. I like to finish with a drizzle of kefir for an added contrast in temperature and a zippy tang."

Seamus Mullen is the owner of El Colmado and Tertulia in New York City and the author of *Seamus Mullen's Hero Food: How Cooking with Delicious Things Can Make Us Feel Better* and *Real Food Heals: Eat to Feel Younger + Stronger Every Day.* Open his fridge and you'll find dark leafy greens, wild blueberries, grass-fed butter, avocados, papaya . . . and kefir.

SERVES 4

½ cup extra virgin olive oil

1 pound large carrots, peeled and cut into 1-inch chunks

1 shallot, finely diced

1 clove garlic, finely diced

1 tablespoon apple cider vinegar

6 cups chicken or vegetable broth

1 teaspoon sea salt

Freshly cracked black pepper

Zest and juice of 1 orange

1 tablespoon grated fresh ginger

¼ teaspoon grated fresh turmeric

1 cup organic plain whole-milk kefir, plus ¼ cup for drizzling

2 tablespoons sunflower seeds, for garnish

4 sprigs fresh dill, for garnish

In a large pot, heat ¼ cup of the olive oil over medium-high heat. Add the carrots and sauté for 5 minutes. Add the shallot and sauté for one more minute, then add the garlic and sauté for another minute. Add the apple cider vinegar to deglaze the pot, using a spoon to stir up any bits stuck to the bottom of the pot. Add the broth and bring everything to a boil, then reduce to a simmer and cook until the carrots are tender, about 20 minutes. Season the soup with the salt and pepper to taste.

Allow the soup to cool slightly and then, working in batches, transfer the soup to a blender with the orange zest and juice, ginger, and turmeric and process at high speed. With the motor running, drizzle in the remaining ¼ cup olive oil and then the kefir.

Divide the soup among four bowls and top each serving with a drizzle of kefir, some sunflower seeds, and sprigs of fresh dill. Serve immediately.

SMALL PLATES

The following small plate concepts hail from as far away as Japan to as close as my home kitchen. These flatbreads, roasted veggies, and other small plates are proof that good things absolutely can come in small packages.

Village Flatbread with Herbed Kefir Farmer Cheese, Eggs, and Tomato

Nearly every culture in the world has its own special take on flatbread. In Ethiopia, spongy, sour injera is torn apart and used to scoop up spicy doro wat (chicken stew) or kik ali-cha (seasoned yellow split peas.) In Armenia, it's tender, crepe-like wraps called lahvosh. There's pita in Greece, naan and chapati in India, tortillas in Mexico . . . that's why I call this my Village Flatbread; every village has one (and I've made it a goal to taste them all). Here, Neapolitan Pizza Crust (page 47) is blanketed with roasted tomatoes, fresh basil, herbed farmer cheese, and sunny-side up eggs. Gather your tribe and take a spin around the world with this traditional pizza Margherita, with a cultured touch.

SERVES 4

FARMER CHEESE

1 cup Kefir Farmer Cheese (page 48)

1 teaspoon chopped fresh thyme

Maldon sea salt

TOMATOES

One 14.5-ounce can whole tomatoes (I like San Marzano)

2 tablespoons plus 1 teaspoon extra virgin olive oil

FLATBREAD

1 ball dough for Neapolitan Pizza Crust (page 47)

10 to 12 small basil leaves

EGGS

4 large brown eggs

Freshly cracked black pepper

FOR THE FARMER CHEESE In a bowl, combine the farmer cheese, thyme, and a pinch of sea salt. Set aside.

FOR THE TOMATOES Preheat the oven to 475°F.

Drain the tomatoes of their liquid, saving the liquid for another recipe. (You can use it in place of the water in the Turkey Chili [page 179] or for any recipe that calls for tomatoes and water.) Toss the tomatoes with 1 tablespoon of the olive oil and a pinch of sea salt and spread them out on a baking sheet. Roast the tomatoes until they brown a bit at the edges, 7 to 10 minutes. Set aside to cool.

FOR THE FLATBREAD Preheat the oven to 525°F. Preheat a pizza stone, cast-iron skillet, or any flat ovensafe surface that retains heat well.

Stretch the pizza dough out as thin as you can on a well-floured surface (preferably a wooden pizza peel). Next, spread the farmer cheese mixture evenly across the surface of the dough, leaving a 1-inch border and making sure not to tear the dough. Evenly distribute the basil leaves on top of the cheese, place the roasted tomatoes evenly across the dough. Bake the pizza on the hot surface until the dough is golden brown, about 4 to 6 minutes. As the pizza is baking, prepare the eggs . . .

FOR THE EGGS In a large nonstick skillet, heat 1 tablespoon of the olive oil over medium-high heat until slightly shimmering. Crack the 4 eggs directly into the pan, being careful to keep their edges separated. Cover the pan with a lid and cook until the whites are set on top but the yolk is still runny, 5 to 6 minutes. Season the eggs with a pinch each of sea salt and pepper.

TO PLATE When the flatbread is done, remove it from the oven and brush the crust border with the remaining 1 teaspoon olive oil (a pastry brush or paper towel works well). Top the flatbread with the eggs and serve.

CHEF'S TIP
An oven setting of 525°F might sound high, but an ultrahot oven in essential for authentic Neapolitan pizza; restaurant-quality wood-fired ovens can cook one in less than 2 minutes! The combination of a very thin crust, soaring temps, and a quick cooking time results in a perfectly puffed crust with little charred hills and paler divots of dough.

Truffle Porcini and Pecorino Cheese Kefir Polenta

Just another attempt to sneak truffles into this cookbook one more time. The struggle is real.

SERVES 4

POLENTA

5 cups water

1 tablespoon kosher salt

1 cup polenta (I like Anson Mills)

2 cups organic plain whole-milk kefir

MUSHROOMS

3 tablespoons extra virgin olive oil

½ pound porcini mushrooms, sliced

FOR SERVING

1 cup grated pecorino cheese

A generous pinch truffle salt, 1 tablespoon truffle oil, or 1 fresh truffle, for garnish

Maldon sea salt (if not using truffle salt for garnish)

> **"La truffe n'est point un aphrodisiaque positif;**
> **mais elle peut, en certaines occasions, rendre les femmes**
> **plus tendres et les hommes plus aimables."**
>
> *"The truffle is not a true aphrodisiac;*
> *but in certain circumstances it can make women*
> *more affectionate and men more attentive."*
>
> —NINETEENTH-CENTURY GOURMAND JEAN-ANTHELME BRILLAT-SAVARIN,
> ONE OF THE MOST INFLUENTIAL FOOD WRITERS OF ALL TIME

FOR THE POLENTA In a large, heavy-bottomed pot, bring the water to a boil and add the kosher salt. Slowly stir in the polenta with a whisk, then reduce to a simmer. Continue stirring this mixture until all of the lumps are smoothed out and the polenta is fully incorporated. Simmer for 45 minutes to 1 hour—the polenta should bubble slightly—stirring occasionally with a wooden spoon. (Be sure to scrape the bottom as you go, to prevent sticking.) Toward the end of the simmering, remove the polenta from the heat and stir in the kefir.

FOR THE MUSHROOMS While the polenta is cooking, in a saucepan, heat the olive oil over medium-high heat. Add the porcinis, evenly distributing them over the bottom of the pot. Let the mushrooms sit, without stirring, until browned, 7 to 10 minutes. (Do not stir them too early; listen for the sizzling sound of moisture evaporating before stirring.) Once the moisture has evaporated, give them a quick stir, then remove the pan from the heat.

TO PLATE Ladle the polenta into a medium/large shallow bowl, topping with the mushrooms and pecorino cheese. Sprinkle the entire platter with the truffle salt or the truffle oil or shave the fresh truffle over it; don't use more than one of these options or it will overpower the dish. If not using truffle salt, sprinkle with a generous pinch of Maldon sea salt.

PROBIOTIC POWER

Polenta contains a type of fiber called insoluble fiber, which travels directly to your gut, where it then ferments, producing multiple strains of probiotics.

Sicilian Fig Bianco with Kefir Farmer Cheese

Ricotta prominently stars in so many Sicilian dishes; you can find it featured on the menu of any cafe or osteria. Perhaps it's because the sheep and cows happily graze on sun-drenched grass growing in the volcanic soil of Mt. Etna, Italy's largest active volcano, or because they spend their days breathing the salty sea air that bathes the island of Sicily.

I think the key to Sicilian cooking is its simplicity. Paring a glorious traditional cheese with leafy greens and local fruits like figs or oranges make me never want to leave the Corleone family's homeland. Here, I pair my farmer cheese, reminiscent of Sicilian ricotta, with sweet, tree-ripe figs for a killer dish that's bound to be a hit.

SERVES 4 TO 6

FARMER CHEESE

1 cup organic plain whole-milk kefir

1 cup Kefir Farmer Cheese (page 48)

1 teaspoon roughly chopped fresh rosemary

Maldon sea salt

PIZZA

1 ball of dough for Neapolitan Pizza Crust (page 47)

8 thin slices prosciutto

1 cup quartered fresh figs

2 teaspoons extra virgin olive oil

FOR SERVING

½ cup arugula

1 teaspoon aged balsamic vinegar

Preheat the oven to 525°F.

FOR THE FARMER CHEESE In a bowl, stir together the kefir, farmer cheese, rosemary, and a pinch of sea salt with a spatula until smooth and spreadable. Set aside.

FOR THE PIZZA Preheat a pizza stone, cast-iron skillet, or any flat ovensafe surface that retains heat well.

Stretch the pizza dough out as thin as you can on a well-floured surface (preferably a wooden pizza peel). Spread the farmer cheese mixture evenly across the pizza dough, leaving a one-inch border and making sure not to tear the dough. Top it with the prosciutto and figs. Bake the pizza on the hot surface until the dough is crispy, 4 to 6 minutes.

Remove the pizza from the oven and brush the edges of the crust with 1 teaspoon of the olive oil (a pastry brush or paper towel works well).

TO PLATE In a bowl, combine the arugula with the remaining 1 teaspoon olive oil, a pinch of sea salt, and the balsamic vinegar. Top the pizza with the dressed arugula and serve.

CHEF'S TIP For authentic, restaurant-quality pizza, at the very end of baking, turn the oven to broil and bring the pizza very close to the broiler for about 5 to 7 seconds; it will brown the top and make the cheese all bubbly and yummy.

Roasted Heirloom Carrots with Cumin and Kefir Labneh

For me, carrots are a sweet, crunchy reminder of my humble peasant roots; of my mother and her five siblings pulling them out of the dirt on her family farm in the Soviet Union; of my grandmother making stew to feed her large family, stretching every harvest and selling the bounty at the local bazaar. Carrots are storytellers, starting out with their roots deep and their gorgeous hue buried beneath the surface. Only with a little help can they be liberated, and it's then, when they're plucked from the dirt, that we can finally understand their journey.

Roasting carrots transforms them from sensible, humble root vegetables into deliciously sweet side dish material. When you envelop moisture-rich veggies like carrots in the dry, hot air of an oven, it concentrates their natural sugars, yielding a bite that's caramelized and a little crunchy on the outside, tender on the inside. Carrots sing to me in warm, harmonious, inviting love notes, like no other vegetable can. Pairing these hardworking veggies with creamy, decadent labneh, feels like a just way to honor them.

SERVES 4

CARROTS

2 bunches small-to-medium unpeeled heirloom carrots

2 tablespoons extra virgin olive oil, plus more for drizzling

1 tablespoon cumin seeds

Maldon sea salt

LABNEH

Kefir Labneh (page 43)

1 tablespoon chopped fresh cilantro

If you've ever dreamed of having clairvoyant abilities, this dish may bring you one step closer. Everyday orange carrots deliver vision-friendly beta-carotene; yellow heirloom carrots have lutein, for even more eye protection. In addition, purple carrots get their groovy shade from memory-enhancing anthocyanins (the same ones that makes eggplants and plums purple), so you'll be able to keep close track of all the cool things you see.

FOR THE CARROTS Preheat the oven to 425°F.

Toss the whole carrots with 1 tablespoon of the olive oil, the cumin seeds, and a pinch of sea salt. Spread the carrots out on a baking sheet and roast until browned and knife-tender, about 20 minutes.

FOR THE LABNEH While the carrots are roasting, in a bowl, mix together the remaining 1 tablespoon olive oil, the labneh, cilantro, and a pinch of sea salt. Let the labneh sit at room temperature while the carrots roast.

TO PLATE Spread the labneh mixture across a family-style platter. Once the carrots have finished, let them cool for about 5 minutes before piling them onto the platter. Drizzle with olive oil and serve warm.

CHEF'S TIPS

If you can't find heirloom carrots, this dish still works beautifully with the orange bunch variety.

VEGGIE ROASTING TIPS

AIM HIGH 15 minutes at 425°F in a standard oven (400°F in a convection oven) will result in a beautifully browned exterior with a soft, tender inside.

BE CONSISTENT Keep your vegetables as uniform in size as possible, whether they're sliced or whole, to ensure they all cook at the same time.

COAT GENEROUSLY with olive oil.

Garlicky Sweet Potato Fries

Besides my mother's Chilled Okroshka (page 176), you won't find a single kefir recipe high-lighting boiled white potatoes.* That's because to me, white potatoes represent everything our family left behind in the Soviet Union: Poverty, oppression, religious persecution. More often than not, my family had very little money, and the only food they could afford was potatoes. So they'd eat them plain, boiled and tossed with butter. Even once we arrived in the United States, my grandmother, Babushka Olga, continued making them; she would babysit my brother and me while my parents worked, and lunch was always boiled potatoes with herring or a pot of boiled potatoes mashed with an entire stick of butter.

That said, there's room on my plate for other kinds of potatoes. I love French fries—the super crispy, crunchy, almost burnt ones. Creamy potato-based soups are lovely as an appe-tizer or light meal. And with sweet potatoes, the whole game changes and I'm in my happy place. Roasting intensifies their flavor by concentrating their naturally occurring sugars; bite through that caramelized crust and you might think you're eating candy.

These "fries" are a heart-healthier take on a dish often found in Russian restaurants, in which white potatoes are sliced into coins with a mandoline, fried in a skillet, and served with a garlicky mayonnaise dip. So good . . . and so unhealthy. Here, I've swapped kefir for the mayo and I roast the sweet potatoes instead of deep-frying them.

The resulting fries still have a little bit of that finger-licking greasiness; a dunk in the garlicky dip provides instant gratification.

SERVES 4

2 large sweet potatoes, cut into French fry-size sticks

2 tablespoons grapeseed oil

½ cup organic plain whole-milk kefir

2 cloves garlic, finely minced

1 teaspoon smoked paprika

1 teaspoon kosher salt

1 teaspoon garlic powder

Pinch of Maldon sea salt

* Okroshka is being grandfathered in, because it's tied to such beloved childhood memories, but even that only calls for a single boiled potato, ultimately divided among four bowls of soup.

Preheat the oven to 425°F.

Toss the sweet potato sticks in the grapeseed oil and spread out evenly across a baking sheet. Bake on one side until browned on the side touching the baking sheet, about 15 minutes. Flip the sticks to the other side and bake until golden brown, an additional 10 minutes.

While the sweet potatoes are roasting, in a bowl, combine the kefir, garlic, paprika, and kosher salt. Set aside.

Transfer the sweet potatoes to a bowl and sprinkle with the garlic powder and Maldon sea salt. Serve warm with the kefir dip.

My mom in Kharkiv's Freedom Square near the statue of Lenin, erected in 1964 and torn down by protesters in 2014.

Latkes

These grated potato pancakes are an iconic Hanukkah dish. Your mouth starts to water the moment you enter the home of someone frying up latkes, as you're enveloped by the perfume of sizzling potatoes and onions. Grating potatoes for just a batch or two is fairly labor intensive; my mom and her employees would grate pound after pound of them, making sure anyone who came to Globus before Hanukkah would be able to purchase what they needed for their latkes.

This version mixes two kinds of potatoes—russets, which fry up extra golden brown and crispy, and sweet potatoes for color—plus parsnips, a root veggie that tastes similar to carrots and gets sweeter as it cooks. Sour cream and applesauce are usually served as toppings; my latkes come with a side of kefir for dunking.

LET MY PEOPLE GLOW

A menorah is lit for eight nights to remind the Jewish people of a miracle that happened in ancient Israel in 165 BCE, when the Jewish Maccabees, celebrating their triumph in a major religious battle, wished to light a flame to rededicate their temple. They had only enough olive oil to fuel the flame for one day. Instead the flame burned for eight days and eight nights. So the latke's symbolism comes not from the potatoes, but from the oil in which they're fried. (Another favorite Hanukkah dish, *sufganiyot*—sugar-dusted jelly-filled doughnuts—are fried in oil, too.)

No matter where we are in the world, during Hanukkah I always bring the menorah and let the light of the season shine bright, reminding our children of their historical and spiritual roots.

DIP

Kefir Labneh (page 43)

1 tablespoon chopped chives

Maldon sea salt

LATKES

1 medium russet potato, peeled and grated

1 medium sweet potato, peeled and grated

1 medium yellow onion, grated

1 medium parsnip, grated

1 clove garlic, peeled and minced

¼ cup chopped fresh parsley

1 teaspoon chopped fresh thyme

1 cup Kefir Ghee (page 41)

FOR THE DIP In a bowl, mix together the labneh, chives, and a pinch of sea salt. Set aside.

FOR THE LATKES In a large bowl, mix the russet potato, sweet potato, onion, parsnip, garlic, parsley, and thyme. Begin forming patties with your hands, using about 1 heaping tablespoon per patty. Set them aside.

In a cast-iron skillet, melt ½ cup of the ghee over medium heat. When the butter shimmers, place as many patties in the skillet as will fit and cook until browned on the bottom side, 5 to 6 minutes. Flip and brown on the other side. When done, remove the latkes from the pan and let them drain on a paper towel. Sprinkle the latkes with a pinch of sea salt. Continue cooking more patties in the remaining ghee until all the latkes are cooked.

TO PLATE Pile the latkes on a platter and serve them with a bowl of the kefir mixture for dipping.

STEP-SAVER Use plain kefir in place of labneh to save time. The dip will be thinner, but it will still deliver a great tang to complement the latkes.

Baked Tostones with Cilantro-Lime Kefir Crema

A tostone is an unripe plantain that has been roasted, sliced, flattened, and fried. Plantains are similar to bananas, but starchier and less sweet. They're not designed to be eaten raw; Mother Nature clearly intended for us to bake them until supple and soft and all of their natural sugar has been coaxed out. Then we smash them into golden bite-size disks, sprinkle them with salt and go to town. Tostones love being dunked into sauces and dips, like this tropical cilantro-lime kefir crema.

SERVES 4

PLANTAINS
4 green plantains
2 tablespoons grapeseed oil
Maldon sea salt

CREMA
2 cups Kefir Labneh (page 43)
1 bunch fresh cilantro, chopped
1 tablespoon taco seasoning
Zest and juice of 2 limes

FOR THE PLANTAINS Preheat the oven to 425°F. Grease a baking sheet.

In a large bowl, toss the whole unpeeled plantains with the grapeseed oil, then place them on a baking sheet and bake until the skin turns black, about 5 minutes. Remove the plantains from the oven and allow them to cool. Once they are cool to the touch, peel and slice the plantains crosswise into ½-inch-thick slices. Use the heel of your hand to gently smash each slice into a flat disk. (Don't press so hard that the plantain becomes very thin; they should still have some thickness to them, almost like a cookie.) Transfer the disks to the baking sheet and bake until crisp, about 20 minutes. Season them with a couple of pinches of sea salt and set them aside in a bowl in a dry, cool place.

FOR THE CREMA In a bowl, combine the labneh, cilantro, taco seasoning, lime zest and juice, and a pinch of sea salt and stir until smooth. Serve with the baked smashed plantains.

Russian Deviled Eggs

Centuries ago, long before sushi went mainstream, Russians introduced the world to the notion of eating fish eggs; black sturgeon caviar was enjoyed by Russia's elite. By the late '70s and early '80s, my parents were selling caviar to satisfy the cravings of the Russian immigrant community: Beluga, Osetra, and Sevruga, plus red ikura caviar—those gorgeous

*red-orange globes that explode in your mouth with salty flavor and texture. They had nego-
tiated an especially phenomenal deal on the red caviar, but it required them to purchase it in
large volumes. For those times when there was a lull in the demand and my parents would
be stuck with too much ikura, Dad had the enterprising idea to sell the excess to local sushi
restaurants, who used it for ikura nigiri, which is seaweed wrapped around a mound of
red fish roe. (Ikura is actually a Japanese word derived from the Russian word for sturgeon
eggs, ikra.) At the time, there were only five sushi bars in Chicago, including Chicago's
first sushi spot, the iconic and legendary Kamehachi, opened by Mrs. Konishi in 1967. My
dad cultivated relationships with all five and once a week, he would drive downtown at 11
o'clock in the evening, after their last customers had cleared out. In the backseat: Me (I was
in kindergarten) and buckets of red caviar. As soon as we walked in and the sushi chefs
saw us, they'd announce, "Konnichiwa, Mike!" As the exchange was made, a chef would fix
me a tamago roll—sweet egg with sticky rice—and Mrs. Konishi would come sit with me,
teaching me how to hold chopsticks and asking me about school or my baby brother. It was
my foray into sushi, which remains one of my favorite meals to this day. As we left, the chefs
would call out, "Arigato, Mike" in unison, and I'd fall asleep in the car on the way home.*

*Deviled eggs, or farshirovanniye yaitsa, are wildly popular and considered a traditional
Russian/Baltic party appetizer. This particular dish fuses Russian and Japanese flavors,
reminding me of those friendly exchanges and the hard work of hungry immigrants with
totally different backgrounds who found a common language in living the American Dream.
Using red caviar in these deviled eggs elevates them to special-occasion status, but they're
so easy and delicious, I could eat them anytime.*

SERVES 6

6 large brown eggs, hard-boiled, peeled, and halved lengthwise
¼ cup organic plain whole-milk kefir
1 teaspoon wasabi paste
1 tablespoon mayonnaise
Pinch of Maldon sea salt
8 teaspoons (4 ounces) red caviar (red salmon roe)
Fresh dill or parsley, for garnish

Remove the yolks from the eggs and place them in a bowl. Mash them with a fork,
then add the kefir, wasabi paste, mayonnaise, and sea salt and mix well. Spoon
the mixture back into the egg whites, topping each egg half with about 1 teaspoon
of caviar. Arrange the deviled eggs on a platter and garnish with the fresh herbs.

ENTREES

When my parents first arrived in the United States more than forty years ago, they cried when they walked into their first American grocery store. There was food stacked from floor to ceiling... seemingly endless amounts of picture-perfect produce, dairy, meats, and even fresh flowers. Our Cold War–era family was used to having to wait in line for hours for a single chicken, only to finally reach the front of the line and learn none were left. America was truly the land of plenty.

Later that first week, strolling through their new Chicago neighborhood, my mom saw a sign outside of a restaurant advertising hot dogs for sale. Using a pocket dictionary to translate those two words, she became terrified of the bizarre foods apparently being consumed here. "Where did you bring me?" she yelled at my father. "They eat dogs here!" Looking back, we all laugh about that story, but I cannot imagine how scared they must have been at all the unknowns, how brave they had to be.

Growing up, my mom was a fabulous cook. She fed us recipes that had been passed down generation to generation, and everything was done by intuition—there were no cookbooks in our kitchen. Because both of my parents were working hard to build our life here, there wasn't always a home-cooked meal on the table (our semifrequent fast-food dinners inspired the Kefir-Battered Cast-Iron Fried Chicken on page 241). But perennial winners like stuffed peppers, stuffed cabbage, and pork dumplings with vinegar and sour cream on the side were always in rotation. And when a holiday or celebration was approaching, Mom would cook for days in advance, pouring her heart and soul into massive lamb roasts and vats of borscht.

The main dishes to come are a reflection of those home-cooked dinners, plus plenty of travel-inspired entrees. A soul-changing experience I had on the beaches of the Yucatan Peninsula coast stands behind the Tulum Grilled Shrimp with Avocado-Kefir Aioli (page 239). The Butter Chicken with Dal and Rice (page 224) is my interpretation of a home-cooked meal I enjoyed while meeting with entrepreneurs at Uganda's Nakivale Refugee Settlement in Uganda. The places I've been, the people I've met while traveling . . . they are all here. I hope these entrees make you feel like you were right alongside me, either on those journeys, or while sitting at my family's dinner table.

Stuffed Peppers

Stuffed peppers take one-pot cooking to a whole new level because you literally eat the cooking vessel. This recipe uses ground beef and rice as a filling, but you can substitute ground turkey, go meat-free with quinoa and sautéed veggies, or improvise with whatever leftovers might be languishing in your fridge.

SERVES 4

FILLING

3 tablespoons extra virgin olive oil

1 pound ground beef (80% lean)

1 large yellow onion, diced

1 clove garlic, minced

1 rib celery, diced

2 medium carrots, unpeeled, 1 diced and 1 grated

1 cup cooked brown or white rice (from ½ cup uncooked)

¼ cup chopped fresh parsley

Maldon sea salt

1 large brown egg

SAUCE

1 cup canned tomato sauce

1 cup organic plain whole-milk kefir

PEPPERS

4 bell peppers, any color

Preheat the oven to 375°F.

FOR THE FILLING In a sauté pan, heat 2 tablespoons of the olive oil over medium heat until slightly shimmering. Add the ground beef and sauté until the beef is browned and cooked through, 5 to 7 minutes. Add half of the diced onion, the garlic, celery, and diced carrot and cook until the vegetables are al dente, 5 to 7 minutes longer.

Transfer the mixture to a bowl, allowing it to cool for a few minutes. Stir in the rice, parsley, 1 teaspoon sea salt, and the egg, mixing thoroughly to incorporate.

FOR THE SAUCE In a saucepan, heat the remaining 1 tablespoon olive oil over medium-high heat. Add the remaining diced onion and sauté until translucent. Add the grated carrot and cook until tender, stirring regularly. Add the tomato sauce and a pinch of sea salt, reduce the heat to low, and simmer for 15 minutes. Remove the pot from the heat. Allow the mixture to cool slightly, then puree until smooth in a blender. Add ½ cup of the kefir and give the sauce a quick pulse in the blender.

FOR THE PEPPERS Cut off the tops of the peppers and discard them. Remove all of the seeds as well as the ribs inside. Shave a little bit off the bottoms of the peppers to make them flat and able to stand up, but not so much as to create any holes. Stuff the peppers with the meat filling, packing it very tightly and allowing it to overflow a bit. Arrange the stuffed peppers standing up in a 10-inch square medium height baking dish. (The dish should be as tall as the peppers.) Fill the dish with as much sauce as you can fit, pouring it over the peppers as well as filling in any gaps in the dish. Bake the peppers until they are soft and cooked through, about 45 minutes.

TO PLATE Divide the stuffed peppers among four shallow soup bowls. Ladle each with a few generous spoonfuls of sauce, followed by a tablespoon or two of kefir, letting it seep in before eating.

Stuffed Cabbage (Golubsti)

Ukrainians and Russians love our golubtsi as much as we love our kefir and our vodka. These babies are labor-intensive, but worth it. You'll get more mileage out of them if you make a large batch and freeze half for later.

SERVES 4

FILLING

4 tablespoons extra virgin olive oil

½ pound ground beef (80% lean)

½ pound ground pork

1 large yellow onion, diced

2 cloves garlic, minced

1 rib celery, diced

1 medium carrot, unpeeled and diced

1 cup cooked brown or white rice (from ½ cup uncooked)

¼ cup chopped fresh parsley

1 teaspoon smoked paprika

Maldon sea salt

1 large brown egg

PROBIOTIC POWER

Cabbage, cauliflower, broccoli, Brussels sprouts, collard greens, kale, turnips, and other cruciferous vegetables are rich sources of *glucosinolates*, sulfur-containing compounds that get broken down by gut microbes to release anti-inflammatory substances that lower the risk of breast, bladder, lung, stomach, liver, and colon cancer.

SAUCE

One 28-ounce can diced tomatoes
(I like San Marzano)

1 cup organic plain whole-milk kefir

1 tablespoon chopped fresh dill

CABBAGE

Kosher salt, for salting the cabbage water

8 to 10 full-size savoy cabbage leaves

"LITTLE DOVES"

According to legend, this dish is called *golubsti* because the little stuffed cabbages resemble doves. The word for *dove* in Russian is голубь, pronounced *golub*. *Golubsti*, then, means "little doves."

Preheat the oven to 375°F.

FOR THE FILLING In a sauté pan, heat 2 tablespoons of the olive oil over medium heat until slightly shimmering. Carefully add the ground beef and pork and sauté until they are browned and cooked through, 5 to 7 minutes. Add half of the diced onion, half of the garlic, the celery, and carrot and cook until the vegetables are al dente, 5 to 7 minutes.

Transfer the mixture to a bowl and let it cool for a few minutes, then stir in the rice, parsley, paprika, 1 teaspoon Maldon salt, and the egg, mixing thoroughly to incorporate.

FOR THE SAUCE In a saucepan, heat 1 tablespoon of the olive oil over medium-high heat. Add the remaining diced onion and garlic and sauté until translucent but not browned, about 5 minutes. Add the tomatoes, reduce the heat to low, and simmer for 15 minutes, adding water as necessary to prevent burning. Remove from the heat and let cool slightly, then transfer to a blender and puree until smooth. Add ½ cup of the kefir and give it a quick pulse in the blender. Lastly, by hand, stir in a pinch of sea salt and the dill.

FOR THE CABBAGE Bring a pot of heavily salted water (it should taste like sea water) to a boil over high heat. Blanch the cabbage leaves in the boiling water for about 1 minute. Remove and drain in a colander, rinsing with cold water to stop the cooking process.

On a cutting board or flat surface, lay out a cabbage leaf, placing about ½ cup of the filling in the center. Wrap the stuffing in the cabbage leaf as you would a burrito. Repeat with the remaining cabbage leaves and stuffing.

In a large Dutch oven, place all the stuffed cabbages in a single layer and cover with the sauce. Cover and bake for 30 minutes. Serve with the sauce.

ROLL WITH IT

Greens make the perfect wrap. Grape leaf–wrapped dolmas; burritos made with giant collard greens; seaweed-wrapped sushi; Asian lettuce wraps . . .

Homemade Gyros with Tzatziki

Whether you've sampled authentic, freshly carved gyros in a Greek taverna or are a connoisseur of food-truck street meat, you know their delicious saltiness and umami. Even though I live in Chicago, I spend a lot of time in New York, for both work and play, and no matter how busy I am, I always carve out time to hit a street vendor and grab a gyro. My favorite guy is parked at Times Square, and there is something so satisfying about watching with anticipation as your meat is piled onto a doughy pita, topped with onions, lettuce, and tomatoes and topped with squiggles of mayo before being handed to you for immediate consumption. It tastes even better after midnight, when you've just left a rubber chicken event and are starving for good food.

This version is a healthier twist on NYC street fare. The gyro meat is homemade, so you know exactly what's going into it, and the kefir tzatziki gives you the same creamy, cool effect as mayonnaise, only lighter.

SERVES 4

1 tablespoon extra virgin olive oil

1 medium yellow onion, finely diced

1 clove garlic, minced

1 teaspoon chopped fresh marjoram

1 teaspoon chopped fresh rosemary

1 teaspoon ground sumac

1 teaspoon Maldon sea salt

1½ pounds ground lamb

4 pitas

1 cup thinly wedged tomatoes

1 cup chopped cucumbers

½ cup diced onion

Tzatziki (page 165)

Parsley, for garnish

Preheat the oven to 325°F.

In a small sauté pan, heat the olive oil over medium-high heat. Add the onion and garlic and cook, stirring to prevent browning, until translucent, about 5 minutes.

Stir in the marjoram, rosemary, sumac, and sea salt. Remove the pan from the heat and allow it to cool. In a bowl, combine the cooled onion mixture with the ground lamb. Pack this mixture firmly into a loaf pan, cover with foil, and place the loaf pan inside a larger baking dish with sides as tall as the loaf pan. Fill the outer baking dish with water that has been heated to 180°F, which is just below a boil. Place everything in the oven and bake until the meat loaf registers an internal temperature of 160°F, 1 hour to 1 hour 15 minutes. Remove from the oven, then remove the lamb from the loaf pan and place it on a cooling rack, weighting it down with a plate or another heavy object until cool.

Slice the loaf thinly and vertically, across the face, with a long carving knife. When done, distribute the meat among the four pitas, topping each with tomato wedges, chopped cucumbers, diced onion, and tzatziki. Garnish with parsley.

Butter Chicken with Dal and Rice

When I arrived at the Nakivale Refugee Settlement in Uganda in 2014, at that point home to nearly sixty thousand refugees, the atmosphere was surprisingly celebratory. Most of these men, women, and children had arrived there after fleeing violence in their homelands of Somalia, Rwanda, and Congo. But now, they were singing and dancing, welcoming my fellow United Nations Foundation Global Entrepreneurs Council members and me as if we were family. The Council was created to advocate and elevate the role of entrepreneurs all over the world, and we were there to observe entrepreneurship in action among locals and refugees. Yes, refugee camps can be full of heartache and despair . . . but if you look deeper, you can often find glimmers of hope, and I was blown away by the intuitiveness and innovation of some of the people we met.

Like Pearl, a thirty-year-old mother of five who had been driven from her home by unspeakable acts of war and violence four years earlier. Pearl had heard of a vocational sewing class being offered at the camp; she signed up and attended twice a week, starting with simple pillowcases and eventually mastering blouses and dresses, which she sold to fellow refugees as well as offsite to shops in town. Within two years, Pearl's profits had grown enough to allow her to purchase five sewing machines, on which she trained a small group of fellow female refugees. Today, their team earns enough to support ten families and the sense of self-reliance has renewed their spirit.

Then there were the members of the Young Mothers Club, who make and sell beautifully scented artisan soap, as well as brooms and baked goods. These were women who, due to an infusion of education about family planning and reproductive health, were learning how to safely space their pregnancies, so they could keep themselves and their babies healthy. Some of them had delivered as many as five babies in five years and had suffered the expected physical, emotional, and financial fallout, but here they were, feeling empowered, happy, proud. They were literally dancing with their babies as they showed us the soaps they had crafted by hand.

For me, a once-inexperienced businesswoman, the experience hit home. Here we were in a place that was designed to be temporary, but had already served as a permanent home to an entire generation of some families. One would expect desperation and pain, but optimism and healing were in bloom. Out of pain came growth; out of scarcity came innovation. Thinkers and doers are everywhere.

The members of our council were treated to an incredible homemade meal. Odongo, a married father of four, had opened a traditional Ethiopian restaurant at Nakivale, featuring the curried chicken stews and spongy sour injera bread of his and his family's homeland. Odongo and his family reminded me a lot of my own parents, desperate to support their families and determined to succeed. That afternoon, we ate rustic, authentic dal—slowly simmered lentils in a savory sauce—at a covered outdoor table, served proudly with a side of hope.

Visiting with the Young Mothers Club in Uganda with the United Nations Foundation Global Entrepreneurs Council with Elizabeth Gore, Ingrid Vandervelt, Devon Kuehne, myself, and Tina Wells (left to right wearing blue hats).

SPICE MIXTURE

¼ teaspoon coriander seeds

Small pinch fenugreek seeds

2 allspice berries

4 black peppercorns

2 cardamom pods

1 whole clove

1 teaspoon smoked paprika

¼ teaspoon cayenne pepper

¼ teaspoon freshly grated nutmeg

¼ teaspoon ground cinnamon

BUTTER CHICKEN

4 tablespoons Cultured Kefir Butter (page 35)

1 teaspoon Maldon sea salt

4 chicken legs, split into thighs and drumsticks

1 tablespoon minced fresh ginger

2 medium red onions, diced

4 cloves garlic, sliced

One 28-ounce can diced tomatoes

4 cups water

DAL AND RICE

2 tablespoons Cultured Kefir Butter (page 35)

4 cardamom pods

1 cup brown basmati or short-grain rice

3 cups cold water

½ cup yellow or red lentils (dal)

1 teaspoon kosher salt

FOR SERVING

¼ cup organic plain whole-milk kefir

FOR THE SPICE MIXTURE In a small skillet over medium heat, gently toast the coriander seeds, fenugreek seeds, allspice, peppercorns, cardamom, and clove until they give off a pleasant aroma, 4 to 6 minutes. Transfer the toasted spices to a spice grinder and grind to a fine powder. (A mortar and pestle will work, too.) Move the ground spices to a bowl and stir in the smoked paprika, cayenne, nutmeg, and cinnamon. Set aside.

FOR THE BUTTER CHICKEN In a large sauté pan, heat the kefir butter over medium heat until it starts to shimmer. Sprinkle in the sea salt, then add the chicken pieces, skin-side down and brown on the first side, 10 to 15 minutes. Once browned, turn the chicken pieces over and add the ginger, red onion, and garlic, making sure that these new ingredients all touch the bottom of the pan and do not rest on top of the chicken pieces. Continue cooking for 4 to 6 minutes.

Add the tomatoes, the spice mixture, and water to the pan with the chicken and simmer over low heat until fully cooked (the chicken should almost fall off the bone), 30 to 40 minutes.

FOR THE DAL AND RICE While the chicken is cooking, in a small sauté pan, melt the kefir butter over medium heat. Add the cardamom and rice and cook for about 4 minutes, stirring occasionally. Add the cold water, dal, and kosher salt. Bring to a soft boil, then reduce to a simmer, cover, and cook for 25 minutes. Remove from the heat and let stand for 15 minutes covered.

TO PLATE Remove the chicken from the sauce and transfer it to a large platter. Pour the sauce over the chicken; drizzle with the kefir. Serve with the dal and rice.

Kefir Jerk Chicken with Mango-Avocado Salsa

This recipe is a Tale of Two Chrisses . . .

SERVES 4

CHICKEN

1 bunch green onions, cut into big pieces

2 Scotch bonnet peppers or habaneros

1 tablespoon grated fresh ginger

2 cloves garlic

1 tablespoon chopped fresh thyme

1 tablespoon ground allspice

1 teaspoon kosher salt

1 cup organic plain whole-milk kefir

2 tablespoons extra virgin olive oil

Juice of 2 limes

1 whole chicken (3½ to 4 pounds), quartered

SALSA

1 mango, pitted, peeled, and diced

1 avocado, pitted, peeled, and diced

1 small red onion, finely diced

1 small jalapeño, seeded and diced

Juice of 2 limes

¼ cup coconut oil

Pinch of Maldon sea salt

¼ cup chopped fresh cilantro

¼ cup chopped fresh mint

At Chris's Kitchen in Oracabessa, Jamaica, owner/chef Chris Sinc-McCalla has been serving up home-cooked Jamaican food and hospitality for nearly two decades. When my family and I wandered into his restaurant, located on the side of the road in the same city where Ian Fleming shacked up to write several James Bond novels, Chef Chris was in the kitchen, tending to a giant batch of jerk chicken. As we chatted, our daughters described snow to his three children and invited their new friends to watch *Frozen* on their iPad with them. "One Love" was playing in the background. The chicken was the perfect balance of spicy, hot, and sweet, a burst of island flavor. Yeah, mon.

CHEF'S TIP The lactic acid in kefir is only mildly acidic, so it works more gently than other acidic marinades. If you have the time, let the chicken (or whatever protein you happen to be working with) bathe in the marinade overnight.

Chris Blackwell is the founder of Island Records. The Rock and Roll Hall of Fame calls him "the single person most responsible for turning the world on to reggae music." Chris is credited with launching Bob Marley's career, along with U2 and Tom Waits. I'm a reggae fiend, so meeting him had me stirring it up, inspiring me to create this version of jerk chicken.

FOR THE CHICKEN In a blender, combine the green onions, Scotch bonnets, ginger, garlic, thyme, allspice, kosher salt, kefir, olive oil, and lime juice and blend until mixed together. Place the chicken quarters in a large roasting pan. Pour the marinade all over the chicken. Cover and marinate in the refrigerator overnight. Thirty minutes before ready to cook, remove the chicken from the refrigerator to come to room temperature.

Fire up your charcoal grill (a grill pan can work, too, but I recommend charcoal for this recipe) and bring to medium heat, about 300°F. (Note: Do not cook the chicken on too high of heat; set up for indirect grilling and keep the heat source about 12 inches away from the chicken.) Shake any excess marinade from the chicken and place the chicken, skin-side down. Keep the grill covered to trap the smokiness. After about 30 minutes, the chicken's skin should be mahogany-colored and the meat should look evenly cooked (a thermometer should read 165°F). Flip the chicken over and finish cooking on the other side, about 10 additional minutes.

FOR THE SALSA While the chicken is cooking, in a bowl, combine the mango, avocado, onion, jalapeño, lime juice, coconut oil, sea salt, cilantro, and mint and toss gently to combine. (Do not overmix this.) Set the salsa aside at room temperature.

FOR YOU Grab a Red Stripe.

TO PLATE Serve the chicken on a large platter, with the salsa on top or served on the side.

Uzbek Shashlik (Kebabs)

For most of my life, I had just one baby brother. I always wanted more siblings; I wanted them so badly, it hurt. When I was twenty-eight, just one year after my father passed away, destiny ushered three new brothers into my life, when my mother married Sasha. At first I was not a happy camper—I was still mourning my father, and the first time I met my new stepfather, I was downright mean. But when I saw how happy he made my mom, when I realized he offered her companionship and friendship, I put my selfish attitude aside and I gave him a shot. Sasha was attentive to my mom's needs; he made her coffee in the morning, brought her flowers every weekend, and proved to be a fabulous, eclectic cook, especially Georgian and Uzbek cuisines, his native heritage.

But what I loved most about our new blended family were my three new brothers, who navigated our merger with grace and maturity. They have since each married lovely, funny, kind brides, as has my biological brother, Eddie. This, combined with a couple of babies, has helped our family grow to epic size. Today, I am surrounded by the siblings I always wanted, yet I didn't have to change a single diaper. Five brothers and four sisters to be exact. I feel blessed to call this Brady Bunch my own. When our loud and crazy mishpucha gathers to break bread for our many celebrations and holidays, one of my favorite meals to share is chef Sasha's Uzbek, kebabs made from ground beef and lamb mixed with onion and cooked on an outdoor grill.

SERVES 4

½ pound ground beef (70% lean)

½ pound ground lamb

1 medium yellow onion, grated

¼ cup chopped fresh parsley

¼ cup chopped fresh cilantro

¼ cup chopped fresh mint

2 teaspoons smoked paprika

1 teaspoon ground cumin

1 teaspoon ground cinnamon

1 teaspoon Maldon sea salt

Pinch of cayenne pepper

Eggplant Baba Ganoush (page 156)

Hummus (page 154)

Tzatziki (page 165)

Pita bread, sliced tomatoes, lemon wedges, and rice pilaf (your favorite)

Soak wooden skewers overnight in cold water.

In a large bowl, combine the meat, onion, herbs, and spices and mix well. Let it stand for 1 hour at room temperature.

Take about 2 heaping tablespoons of the beef and lamb mixture and shape it into a flat sausage shape. Slide a skewer lengthwise through the middle of the kebab, repeating until all the kebabs have been skewered.

Fire up your outdoor grill to very hot. Wipe the grill grates with a bit of oil and grill the kebabs on one side, making sure they brown and do not stick to the grill, 4 to 6 minutes. Flip the kebabs and finish cooking until cooked medium, about 4 minutes. (If you don't have an outdoor grill, you can use a grill pan or cast-iron skillet.)

Serve with tzatziki, hummus, baba ghanoush, pita bread, sliced tomatoes, lemon wedges, and your favorite rice pilaf.

Lula Café
Kefir Chicken

Tzatziki

Uzbek Shashlik
(Kebabs)

Lula Café Kefir Chicken

RECIPE COURTESY OF JASON HAMMEL

You've never had chicken as juicy as this. When you soak poultry or meat in kefir overnight, it acts as a natural tenderizer, resulting in chicken that is ridiculously moist. (That's why tandoori chicken is marinated in yogurt before moving to the clay oven, and why traditional fried chicken is first dipped in buttermilk before dredging.) This recipe comes courtesy of my friend Jason Hammel, chef and owner of Lula Café in Chicago's Logan Square neighborhood. Lula was far ahead of its time; it opened in 1999, highlighting seasonable, sustainable, farm-to-table dining before that was the hipster thing to do. Almost twenty years later—an eternity in restaurant years—it's still packed from breakfast through dinner. Dishes like this marinated chicken with grapes and Marcona almonds are one reason why.

Chef Hammel is also a founding member of Pilot Light, a not-for-profit organization devoted to writing a food-based curriculum for Chicago Public Schools with the goal of helping children make healthier choices by connecting the lessons they learn in their classrooms to the foods they eat on their lunch trays, at home, and in their communities.

SERVES 4

OVERNIGHT MARINADE

4 organic boneless, skin-on chicken breasts

Kosher salt and freshly cracked black pepper

3¼ cups organic plain whole-milk kefir

Zest of 2 lemons

3 teaspoons chopped fresh oregano

LEEKS

4 large leeks

4 tablespoons Cultured Kefir Butter (page 35)

2 splashes vermouth

CHICKEN

1 tablespoon extra virgin olive oil

SAUCE

A handful green grapes

½ cup Marcona almonds, chopped

1 small head radicchio endive, cut into 1-inch segments

Pinch of sea salt

½ lemon

FOR THE OVERNIGHT MARINADE The day before you plan to serve this chicken, start by marinating it. Heavily season both sides of the chicken breasts with kosher salt and black pepper. In a bowl, whisk together 3 cups of the kefir, the lemon zest, and 2 teaspoons of the oregano. Place the chicken in the bowl with the marinade, turning to coat. Wrap the container with plastic wrap so it's airtight and refrigerate it overnight.

FOR THE LEEKS When you are ready to begin cooking, cut the leeks lengthwise, rinse out any dirt, and slice them into thin, julienne strips.

In a sauté pan, melt 2 tablespoons of the kefir butter over low heat. Add the leeks and begin to cook, stirring occasionally. As the leeks melt down, a good amount of water will evaporate from them; when they finally stop steaming, add a splash of vermouth. Continue cooking until the alcohol has cooked out, a minute or two. Set aside.

FOR THE CHICKEN Preheat the oven to 350°F.

In a large ovenproof skillet, big enough for all 4 chicken breasts, heat the olive oil over medium heat. Remove the chicken from the marinade and pat the breasts dry with paper towels to prevent any oil from sputtering when they're added to the pan (discard the marinade). Place the chicken in the skillet, skin side down, and allow the skin to sear and become crispy and golden before trying to pick the chicken up, about 5 minutes. Flip the chicken and place the skillet in the oven. After 15 to 20 minutes, check the chicken for doneness by feeling for firmness and looking for visual signs like white flesh and clear juices coming out of it.

FOR THE SAUCE Once the chicken is cooked, remove it from the skillet and set aside somewhere warm while you hold on to the skillet to make the sauce. First, drain the fat from the pan. Place the skillet back on the stove over medium heat. Add a little more vermouth to deglaze the pan. Reduce the liquid to a nappe consistency—thin enough to coat the back of a spoon. This will take 1 to 2 minutes and will reduce the liquid by half. Then add the braised leeks. Add the grapes and let them gently simmer until they just start to pop. Add the remaining 2 tablespoons kefir butter and remove the pan from the heat, stirring it into the leeks. Add the chopped Marcona almonds, the endive, sea salt, a squeeze of lemon, and the remaining 1 teaspoon oregano and ¼ cup kefir and stir everything gently.

TO PLATE Slice the chicken breasts and divide them among four plates, spooning the sauce over the top.

Sayulita Fish Tacos with Cabbage Slaw

Sayulita, Mexico, is paradise for surfers, artists, yogis, beach bums, and adventurers alike. When I'm there, I let my bohemian freak flag fly: Straw fedora, mala prayer beads, espadrilles, pom-pom tote bag. Every square inch of downtown is saturated with color, art, and Frida Kahlo–inspired merchandise . . . vibrant flag banners crisscross the streets; pigment-soaked murals feature everything from hamsas to Day of the Dead skulls; street performers toss flaming batons in the air. The neighborhoods look like a box of crayons exploded, leaving fuchsia, tangerine, aqua, and purple homes in its wake.

Whether you're sitting at a popular outdoor bar just steps from the ocean or stopped at a roadside stand with a giant umbrella and no menu, order the fish tacos. At our favorite spot, The Real Fish Taco, that's pretty much all you can order; they come grilled or fried, made with fresh-caught marlin or mahi-mahi. My Sayulita Fish Tacos—crispy fish fingers topped with crunchy kefir slaw—are a tribute to this sunny boho sweet spot.

SERVES 4

FISH

1 pound cod, haddock, red snapper, or other white fish (avoid tilapia)

1 cup whole wheat flour

1 tablespoon kosher salt

1 teaspoon ground cumin

1 teaspoon chili powder

2 cups organic plain whole-milk kefir

2 cups grapeseed oil

CABBAGE SLAW

1 cup shredded red cabbage

1/2 red onion, sliced

1/2 cup shredded carrots

1 cup fresh cilantro leaves

Pinch of Maldon sea salt

FOR SERVING

8 corn tortillas

1 avocado, sliced

Sliced jalepeño chilis

FOR THE FISH Cut the fish into finger-size pieces and pat dry. In one bowl, combine the flour, kosher salt, cumin, and chili powder. In another bowl, add 1½ cups of the kefir. Gently place all of the fish into the bowl of kefir.

While the fish marinates, in a cast-iron skillet or sauté pan, heat the grapeseed oil to 360°F (use a thermometer or throw a little bit of flour into the oil; it should fry right up). Piece by piece, take the fish out of the kefir and dredge it in the seasoned flour, shaking off any excess flour, and carefully drop it into the hot oil. Cook each piece until it reaches a medium-dark brown, about 4 minutes per side. Drain on paper towels. Complete the process until all the fish is cooked (discard any remaining marinade).

FOR THE CABBAGE SLAW In a medium bowl, combine the cabbage, onion, carrots, cilantro, sea salt, and remaining ½ cup kefir. Let it sit for 15 minutes.

TO PLATE Heat the tortillas over a grill or steam them with tongs over a pot of boiling water, wrapping them in a kitchen towel as you go to keep them moist and warm. Divide warm tortillas among four plates, topping with the fish and the slaw. Serve with the sliced avocado and chilis.

Follow your heart to boho Hotel Hafa in Sayulita, Mexico.

Tulum Grilled Shrimp
with Avocado-Kefir Aioli
(top) and Sayulita Fish
Tacos with Cabbage Slaw
(bottom)

Tulum Grilled Shrimp with Avocado-Kefir Aioli

When you're at a midnight bongo drum circle on the beach in Tulum, Mexico, and the DJ starts spinning electronica, there's only one thing to do: Dance. So when I found myself in that exact, surreal situation, I immediately set my purse down on a nearby drum and started jamming. With me were two hundred of my closest friends; we were in Tulum for Summit Series, an annual pilgrimage of entrepreneurs, thought leaders, activists, and philanthropists, gathering to speak, listen, collaborate, and grow.

The drum circle was set in the bottom of a cenote—essentially a giant sinkhole. We danced until three o'clock in the morning, at which point I went back to the drum to grab my purse.

No purse.

It was gone, along with all of the bongos. (To this day, I truly feel the band accidentally packed my bag up with their equipment; I refuse to believe it was stolen.) My first thought: "Oh my God, my phone." My photos. My contacts. Notes I'd been making for this book. My last backup had been four months prior. Not to mention the fact that my wallet was in there, too.

Then I remembered that while on the flight to Tulum, when I was feeling stressed out and tired, I had calmed myself down by telling the universe, "I'm open to this trip. I don't have time for it, but I'm open. Just give me what I need. I have no expectations."

Maybe a painful forced digital detox was exactly what the universe felt I needed.

My purse never did show up. But losing it taught me some valuable lessons:

- *There are always good-hearted people around who will help you in your time of need. (Friends and Summit Series staff loaned me money, shared their food, and let me use their phones to make arrangements.)*

- *Most of the things you can accomplish on your iPhone, you can accomplish with a journal and pen, too.*

- *When the universe wants you to pause, it will find a way to make you pause.*

This Tulum grilled shrimp recipe was served at a beachside dinner, just hours before that fateful drum circle.

SERVES 4

DRESSING

1 bunch cilantro

Avocado Kefir Goddess Dressing (page 148)

SHRIMP

2 pounds large (16–20 count) shrimp, peeled and deveined, tails on

Zest and juice of 2 limes

1 teaspoon ground cumin

Pinch of chili flakes

1 teaspoon Old Bay seasoning

FOR SERVING

1 head romaine lettuce, quartered

2 large avocados, peeled, pitted, and diced

Lemon or lime wedges, for garnish

FOR THE DRESSING Cut off the cilantro stems and roughly chop them. (Set the leaves aside for garnish.) In a blender, combine the chopped stems and dressing and blend until smooth. Place in the refrigerator while preparing the shrimp.

FOR THE SHRIMP In a bowl, combine the shrimp with the lime zest, lime juice, cumin, chili flakes, and Old Bay and marinate, refrigerated, for 2 hours.

Fire up your outdoor grill to very hot. Wipe the grill grates with a bit of oil and grill the shrimp over high heat, flipping halfway through and cooking until done. (If you don't have an outdoor grill, you can use a grill pan or cast-iron skillet.)

TO PLATE Place a romaine quarter on each of four plates. Top each with some goddess dressing, chopped avocado, grilled shrimp, and a little more dressing. Garnish with the cilantro leaves and lemon or lime wedges.

Kefir-Battered Cast-Iron Fried Chicken

Adjusting to life in America meant eating traditional American foods, and Colonel Sanders made that an easy task, indeed. After a long day at work, my mom, too tired to cook, would often return home with one of those iconic red-and-white buckets stacked to the brim with fried chicken. (And biscuits. And mashed potatoes. And buttery corn.) First, we would peel the skin off, savoring its crispy, salty texture before biting into the moist meat while the man with the white beard smiled at me from the pail. Delish.

Now, when a craving for fried chicken hits, I turn to this recipe, which tastes nothing like chicken that's been passed through a fast-food window—and that's a good thing. The chicken is marinated overnight in kefir, so the lactic acid helps tenderize it while imparting a subtle buttermilk flavor. It's fried in grapeseed oil, which is high in polyunsaturated fats and vitamin E, plus has a high smoke point, making it a nice substitute for olive or vegetable oils when frying (sautéing and stir-frying, too). The result: an incredibly juicy piece of fried chicken that's still somehow good for you.

If you really want to go all-in, serve this atop a pile of waffles (page 70), drizzling rich Salt and Pepper Maple Syrup (page 243) over the whole shebang.

SERVES 4 TO 6

1½ cups organic plain whole-milk kefir

1 cup kosher salt

1 whole organic chicken (about 3 pounds)

1½ cups grapeseed oil

1 cup panko breadcrumbs, crushed

½ cup organic whole wheat flour

1 tablespoon smoked paprika

1 teaspoon freshly cracked black pepper

1 teaspoon cayenne pepper

Pinch of Maldon sea salt

In a bowl, mix the kefir with ½ cup of the kosher salt. Set aside.

Trim and cut the chicken into 10 pieces: 2 drumsticks; 2 thighs; 2 wings; and 2 breasts, each cut in half (leave the breasts on the rib cage). Pat all the pieces dry with a paper towel, then add the chicken to the kefir mixture. Cover and let sit overnight in the refrigerator. When ready to cook, pull the bowl out of the refrigerator about 30 minutes prior to cooking.

Preheat the oven to 425°F. Set a wire rack in a rimmed baking sheet near the stove.

Place a 9-inch cast-iron pan on the stovetop and pour in the grapeseed oil. Begin warming the oil over medium-high heat.

In a bowl, mix together the panko, flour, paprika, black pepper, cayenne, and remaining ½ cup kosher salt.

Remove one piece of chicken at a time from the kefir marinade and dredge it in the panko/flour mixture, making sure that all surfaces are covered. Lift the piece of chicken up, gently shake it off, and place on a plate. Repeat until all chicken pieces are coated.

Take a small amount of the panko/flour mixture and place it in the hot oil in the cast-iron pan. It should bubble up around the sides and brown slowly. If it browns too quickly, turn the heat down and wait a few minutes and try again. If it does not bubble at all, turn the heat up, wait a few minutes and try again.

Once the oil is at the right temperature, place about half of the chicken pieces in the pan, leaving room between the pieces. You should be able to fry all the chicken in two batches. When one side of a piece of chicken is brown, 7 to 10 minutes, gently flip it in the pan using tongs or a slotted spatula. Repeat on the other side until golden brown. Remove each piece from the pan once browned and place on the rack in the baking sheet. Repeat until all pieces are browned. Place the baking sheet pan in the oven and bake for about 15 more minutes. Remove from the oven and sprinkle each piece with a touch of sea salt.

NOTE Don't worry too much about the salt in this recipe—most of it will be left behind in the marinade bowl.

Salt and Pepper Maple Syrup

MAKES 1 CUP

1 cup dark amber maple syrup
2 tablespoons freshly cracked black pepper
Pinch of Maldon sea salt

In a small saucepan, combine the maple syrup, pepper, and salt and bring to a gentle simmer for about 3 minutes. Remove from the heat and set in a warm spot until ready to serve over the chicken and waffles.

Farmer Cheese and Veggie Stuffed Lasagna

I love baking lasagna at home. I make mine with layers of thinly sliced zucchini and mushrooms; they give the dish a meaty texture without weighing it down. Instead of ricotta, I use farmer cheese. It's oven-baked Italian comfort food at its best.

SERVES 4 TO 6

SAUCE

3 tablespoons extra virgin olive oil

2 cloves garlic, sliced

1 medium yellow onion, diced

1 tablespoon chopped fresh basil

One 28-ounce can whole peeled tomatoes (I like San Marzano)

FARMER CHEESE

1½ cups Kefir Farmer Cheese (page 48)

1 large brown egg, separated

1 teaspoon kosher salt

TO ASSEMBLE

12 lasagna noodles, cooked

1 green zucchini, thinly sliced

1 yellow zucchini, thinly sliced

1 cup sliced mushrooms

1 cup shredded mozzarella cheese

Preheat the oven to 375°F.

FOR THE SAUCE In a large sauté pan, heat 2 tablespoons of the olive oil over medium-high heat until slightly shimmering. Add the garlic, onion, and basil and cook until the onion is translucent, about 5 minutes. Add the tomatoes and simmer over medium heat for about 45 minutes.

FOR THE FARMER CHEESE In a bowl, mix together the farmer cheese, egg yolk, and kosher salt. Set aside.

TO ASSEMBLE Pour a little sauce into the bottom of a 9 x 12-inch square pan, topping it with three cooked lasagna noodles placed side by side. Top the noodles with half the farmer cheese, then another layer of noodles. Top with the green and yellow zucchini, mushrooms, and about half of the tomato sauce. Add another layer of noodles, the remaining farmer cheese, and a final layer of noodles. Top it all off with the remaining tomato sauce and the mozzarella. Bake until the cheese is bubbling and golden brown, about 30 minutes.

TIP If you know someone who recently had a baby or has been feeling unwell, make two of these lasagnas at the same time and bring one over. They freeze and reheat easily.

Farmer Cheese and Arugula Stuffed Shells with Meat Sauce

For a twist on lasagna, I tinkered with my standard recipe and stuffed it into some oversize pasta shells. You get the same classic Italian flavors and textures—fragrant basil and garlic, sweet tomato sauce, melty cheese, tender noodles—only in a different form.

SERVES 4

SAUCE

3 tablespoons extra virgin olive oil

½ pound ground beef (80% lean)

2 cloves garlic, sliced

1 medium yellow onion, diced

1 tablespoon chopped fresh basil

3 teaspoons Maldon sea salt

One 28-ounce can whole peeled tomatoes (I like San Marzano)

SHELLS

1½ cups Kefir Farmer Cheese (page 48)

1 cup chopped arugula

1 large brown egg yolk

8 extra-large (jumbo) pasta shells, cooked

½ cup freshly shredded Parmigiano-Reggiano cheese

Preheat the oven to 375°F.

FOR THE SAUCE In a large sauté pan, heat 2 tablespoons of the olive oil over medium-high heat until slightly shimmering. Add the ground beef and cook until browned, 5 to 7 minutes. Add the garlic, onion, basil, and 2 teaspoons of the salt and cook until the onion is translucent, about 5 minutes. Add the tomatoes and simmer over medium heat for about 45 minutes.

FOR THE SHELLS In a bowl, combine the farmer cheese, arugula, egg yolk, the remaining 1 tablespoon olive oil and 1 teaspoon salt. Stuff each shell with about ¼ cup of the cheese mixture.

TO BAKE Arrange the stuffed shells in a baking dish, seam-side down. Cover with the meat sauce, top with the Parmigiano-Reggiano cheese, and bake until the cheese is bubbling and golden brown, about 30 minutes.

Wild Cod with Black Olive, Fennel, and Orange

Black olive, fennel, and orange is a classic flavor combination. Fennel's licorice flavor pairs well with sweet orange segments; olives add a briny, savory punch.

SERVES 4

DRESSING
1 bulb fennel
¼ cup organic plain whole-milk kefir
Juice of 1 lemon
2 teaspoons Maldon sea salt
1 cup black olives, pitted
2 oranges, peeled and supremed (I like Cara Cara or blood oranges)

FISH
1 large wild cod fillet (about 1½ pounds)
2 tablespoons extra virgin olive oil

Cut the fronds off of the fennel bulb and set them in an ice bath. Cut the bulb in half, discard the core, then use a mandoline or very sharp knife to shave what remains. Add the fennel shavings to the ice bath and let sit about 1 hour. (This will help keep the fennel nice and crisp.)

Preheat the oven to 400°F. Place a large roasting pan inside to preheat.

FOR THE DRESSING In a bowl, whisk together the kefir, lemon juice, and 1 teaspoon of the sea salt. Stir in the black olives and orange segments. Remove the shaved fennel from the ice water, pat it dry, and add it to the dressing. Set aside.

FOR THE FISH Season the fish with the remaining 1 teaspoon sea salt. Remove the preheated roasting pan and add the olive oil, spreading it to coat. Place the fish on top and roast until white and flaky, about 15 minutes. Remove the fish from the oven, transfer it to a large platter, and top with the fennel mixture. Drain the chopped fennel fronds, roughly chop them, and scatter them across the platter before serving.

Kielbasa Sausage with Pickled Red Onion and Kefir Dip

Mom put my brother and me to work at her deli on days when we didn't have school; I was responsible for sticking price tags on various foods, ringing and bagging groceries, restocking shelves, and sweeping the floors. Globus Deli was always buzzing, a rotating cast of Ukrainian and Russian characters filtering in and out in search of a taste of their homeland. Besides kefir, we had delicacies like Bulgarian candies, imported raw cheeses, jars of plum butter (my favorite!), and sour cherry compote. My mom was lightning quick with her abacus, the black beads whizzing by on the little metal rods, click click click, as she tallied up her customers' bills.

An elderly immigrant named Faina worked in the back of the deli, rolling out dough for pirozhki dumplings all day long. (She was our Saturday night babysitter, too.) A lean, scrappy man who worked for a local blanket company used to come in all the time with feathers stuck in his giant beard; his nickname was Gryazny, which loosely translates to "dirty." I was terrified of him; I'd hide behind the counter, crying, praying that Gryazny didn't call my name. Very often, customers would purchase an expensive whole fish, eat half of it, then bring it back, bones and all, claiming it was spoiled in an effort to recoup their money. My mother would tell them, in more colorful terms than this, to stop bothering her.

For Eddie and me, Globus Deli was our personal playground. While other kids were playing video games and having sleepovers, my brother and I were at Globus, having a ball while helping our mother establish her career and build our life in America. Over the years, she amassed a collection of imported Belgian butter crisps, Russian zefir (marshmallows), chocolate-covered plums, and other European candies, and we reaped the benefits. When we were bored, we'd chase each other around the store with smoked taranka—smoked, salted dried fish that Russians usually chase with beer—pretending we had cooties.

Giant kielbasa sausages hung over the front counter at Globus, and their smoky, salty smell permeated the store. When my mom, brother, and I returned home, we'd smell like kielbasa, too. Even now, thirty-five years later, if I see kielbasa on a menu, I'm instantly transported right back to Globus, and I smile.

ONIONS

2 cups water

1 teaspoon sugar

1 tablespoon kosher salt

1 bunch fresh thyme

2 cloves garlic

2 cups red wine vinegar

1 medium red onion, cut into eighths

KIELBASA

4 kielbasa links (4 to 6 ounces each)

2 tablespoons extra virgin olive oil

CHILI-FENNEL LABNEH

Pinch of chili flakes

1 teaspoon fennel seeds

½ cup organic plain whole-milk kefir

Kefir Labneh (page 43)

Pinch of Maldon sea salt

FOR THE ONIONS In a small saucepot, bring the water to a boil over high heat. Add the sugar, kosher salt, thyme, and garlic and remove from the heat, allowing the mixture to cool. Once cool, stir in the vinegar. Place the red onions in a bowl and pour the vinegar mixture over them. Let sit at room temperature for an hour (although you could let them pickle overnight, too).

FOR THE KIELBASA Score the kielbasa with a paring knife. Fire up your outdoor grill to very hot. Wipe the grill grates with a bit of oil and grill the kielbasa on high, about 3 minutes per side. (If you don't have an outdoor grill, heat 1 tablespoon of the olive oil in a skillet over medium heat until slightly shimmering. Add the kielbasa and cook until evenly browned all over, 5 to 7 minutes.)

FOR THE CHILI-FENNEL LABNEH In a small skillet, toast the chili flakes and fennel seeds over medium heat until they give off a pleasant aroma, 2 to 3 minutes. Remove the pan from heat and allow to cool. Blend the spices in a spice grinder or with a mortar and pestle.

In a bowl, combine the ground spices, kefir, labneh, Maldon salt, and the remaining 1 tablespoon olive oil.

TO PLATE Divide the kielbasa links among four plates, along with some drained red onions and chili-fennel labneh.

My mom auditing a store clerk at a grocery store she worked at in the Soviet Union.

Pan-Seared Salmon Burgers with Tzatziki

These flavor-packed salmon patties are light, bright, and so good for you. Salmon is naturally abundant in heart-healthy fats and protein; wild salmon, in particular, offers the literal ABCs of vitamins (vitamins A, B3, B12, C, D, and E). In our family, we eat these bunless, and topped with thick tomato slices, avocado, and tzatziki, but you can trick them out in all sorts of ways: On a soft brioche bun with Avocado Kefir Goddess Dressing (page 148), Po' boy-style; in a mixed green salad, or wrapped in steamed collard greens.

SERVES 4

1 pound ground wild salmon

2 large brown eggs

¼ cup minced shallots

1 teaspoon chopped fresh dill

Juice of ½ lemon

Maldon sea salt

2 tablespoons extra virgin olive oil

4 brioche buns

Tzatziki (page 165)

Lemon wedges, for squeezing

In a bowl, combine the salmon, eggs, shallots, dill, lemon juice, and a pinch of sea salt. Form the salmon mixture into 4 equal patties.

In a cast-iron skillet, heat the olive oil over medium heat. Once the oil is slightly shimmering, place the patties in the skillet and cook on one side until browned, 3 to 4 minutes. Flip the patties and finish cooking on the other side, then remove the skillet from the heat.

Divide the salmon burgers among four buns, topping each with tzatziki. Season very lightly with sea salt and a squeeze of lemon juice.

Garlicky Sweet Potato Fries

Hummus

Falafel Sandwiches

You can throw these addictive Middle Eastern chickpea balls in anything and it will taste good: Salad, a pita or wrap, a bowl of hummus. Besides its versatility, this authentic Mediterranean treat is vegetarian, gluten-free, and offers lots of fiber and protein. Be sure to start with dried chickpeas, and soak but don't cook them. Cooking them will result in a mushy falafel, as will using canned chickpeas.

SERVES 4 TO 6

1 cup dried chickpeas

4 cups cold water

1 clove garlic, minced

¼ red onion, grated

1 teaspoon ground coriander

1 teaspoon ground cumin

1 teaspoon smoked paprika

¼ cup chopped fresh parsley

¼ teaspoon baking soda

1 teaspoon kosher salt

Grapeseed oil, for frying

4 pitas

Tzatziki (page 165)

1 cup shredded red cabbage

1 cup chopped tomatoes

½ cup diced red onions

Hummus, for serving (page 154)

Soak the chickpeas for 24 hours in the cold water. Drain well.

In a food processor, combine the soaked chickpeas, garlic, onion, coriander, cumin, paprika, parsley, baking soda, and salt. Pulse-chop the mixture, being careful not to puree it. (You want a chunky consistency.) Add water tablespoon by tablespoon, adding just enough to bring the mixture together.

Pour at least 3 inches of oil into a large, deep pot and heat over medium-high heat to 350°F.

Scoop about 1 heaping tablespoon of the falafel mixture at a time, shaping it into a ball before carefully dropping it into the frying oil. Fry until browned, 4 to 6 minutes. Remove the falafel from the oil and drain in a bowl lined with a paper towel.

Divide the pita among four plates. Stuff each one with some falafel, tzatziki, shredded cabbage, chopped tomatoes, and diced red onions. Serve with hummus.

Red Snapper Open-Faced Sandwiches

Seasoning red snapper with sugar, salt, and fennel seed before sautéing it in kefir butter will give you one of the most flavorful pieces of fish you've ever had the pleasure of eating.

SERVES 6 TO 8

SPREAD

¼ cup chopped fresh dill, plus extra for garnish

2 teaspoons capers, rinsed and drained

½ cup Kefir Labneh (page 43)

FISH

1 teaspoon sugar

1 teaspoon kosher salt

1 teaspoon fennel seeds

¼ cup Cultured Kefir Butter (page 35)

2 skinless red snapper fillets (10 to 12 ounces each)

FOR SERVING

6 to 8 slices 7-seeded grain bread

1 heirloom tomato, cut into ¼-inch-thick slices

1 medium red onion, shaved on a mandoline and reserved in ice water

Pinch of freshly cracked black pepper

FOR THE SPREAD In a bowl, combine the dill, 1 teaspoon capers, and labneh. Set aside.

FOR THE FISH In a small bowl, combine the sugar, salt, and fennel seeds. Use this mixture to lightly season the fish.

In a large sauté pan, melt the kefir butter over medium-high heat. Carefully add the snapper fillets, laying them down away from you, and cook the fish until just barely done, 3 to 4 minutes. Flip and continue cooking for another 3 to 4 minutes. Remove the fish from the pan and set aside on a large plate. Divide the fish into 6 to 8 pieces.

TO PLATE Toast the bread. Immediately smear each piece with some of the labneh spread, then layer with the tomato, fish, and onion. Sprinkle the remaining 1 teaspoon of capers, a little dill, and the black pepper on top and serve.

Grilled Trout with Fermented Cabbage and Beets

Placing a whole, grilled trout on the table makes for a lovely showpiece, but the homemade beet sauerkraut is the real star here. When you submerge cabbage—or beets, or cucumbers, or any vegetable, really—in salt water, a kind of magic happens, where the bacteria that naturally reside on the leaves start to break down the cabbage into an easier-to-digest form. Those bacteria produce carbon dioxide and lactic acid. Soon enough, the environment becomes too acidic for the original bacteria to survive; they bid the world a fond farewell, and are replaced with good-for-you probiotic bacteria.

It takes time (you'll want to start the cabbage portion of this recipe 1 to 3 weeks before you're ready to eat it), but it's worth the effort; kraut made from scratch is crunchy, pungent, tangy, full of flavor, and (literally) tingles your tongue with probiotics. Celebrity integrative physician Andrew Weil, MD, has even called it "a living food."

FERMENTATION NATION

David Chang of Momofuku fame has described fermentation as, "When rotten goes right." I couldn't have said it better myself. Once relegated to the back of health food stores, fermented foods—foods that have been inoculated with microorganisms that convert their naturally occurring sugar to acids, gases, or alcohol—are enjoying a renaissance. I'm not just talking about kefir; probiotic foodie darlings like kombucha, black garlic, miso, kimchi, artisanal sauerkrauts, and fermented salsa are on all the hottest menus right now. They don't even need to be that exotic sounding; beer, pickles, and soy sauce are all fermented foods that might be in your fridge at this very moment.

Not only does fermentation lead to the birth of billions of happy, flavorful bacteria, it amplifies whatever vitamins and nutrients are already in the food. So in the case of the beet sauerkraut (page 264), the vitamin B6, vitamin C, potassium, and folate present in both the cabbage and the beets are somewhat ignited during the fermentation process.

Including fermented foods besides kefir, like sauerkraut and kimchi, is also a smart way to diversify your microflora—the community of bacteria living in your gut. The more diversity you have in your GI tract, the better protected you may be against all sorts of diseases. That's because the specific strains of probiotics found in, say, miso soup, tempeh, or other plant-based foods, may be more effective at reducing the risk of different diseases than the strains found in fermented dairy.

BEET SAUERKRAUT

1 head napa cabbage

5 red beets, peeled and shredded on a mandoline

3 tablespoons plus 2 pinches Maldon sea salt

DRESSING

¼ cup organic plain whole-milk kefir

1 teaspoon ground cumin

1 tablespoon chopped fresh basil

¼ cup extra virgin olive oil

FISH

2 whole trout (about ½ pound each)

1 tablespoon all-purpose flour

Zest of 1 lemon

FOR SERVING

Juice of 1 lemon

2 tablespoons grapeseed oil

FOR THE BEET SAUERKRAUT Quarter the cabbage and cut out and discard the tough core from each wedge. Chop the cabbage into ½-inch-wide slices and add them to a bowl with the shredded beets. Toss the cabbage and beets with 2 tablespoons of the sea salt. Use your clean hands to knead and squeeze the vegetables with the salt for 10 to 15 minutes, taking frequent rests to let the juices seep out of the produce. Transfer everything to a ½-gallon mason jar, making sure the cabbage and beets are submerged in the brine. (Try to leave 1 inch of space or more between the top of the liquid and the top of the jar, as the vegetables will expand as they ferment.) Screw the lid on the jar and leave it, unrefrigerated, in a cool, dark area for 1 to 3 weeks, after which you should refrigerate it.

FOR THE DRESSING In a bowl, combine the kefir, cumin, basil, olive oil, and remaining 1 tablespoon sea salt. Pull the fermented cabbage and beets out of their liquid and toss them with the kefir dressing. Set aside.

FOR THE FISH Sprinkle the trout with the flour and season with a pinch of sea salt and the lemon zest. In a large sauté pan, heat the grapeseed oil over medium heat. Once the oil is slightly shimmering, add the trout and cook until crisp and cooked all the way through, 4 to 6 minutes per side.

TO PLATE When the fish is ready, transfer it to a platter and top it with the beet sauerkraut, a liberal squeeze of lemon juice, and a pinch of sea salt.

SWEET ON TART

As people move away from salt and sugar for health reasons, an unexpected flavor sensation has been rising in the ranks. Tart, sour flavors are stimulating, bright, and they lend sparkle and a new dimension of flavor to your dishes. Naturally tart foods like kefir, tart cherries, grapefruit, tamarind, kombucha, and drinking vinegars also come with science-backed health credentials: Tart foods tend to be high in various acids that can enhance nutrient absorption (citric acid in grapefruit increases iron availability; lactic acid in kefir maximizes calcium absorption). Many tart foods get their sour tang from fermentation, meaning the tang you taste comes from all those helpful bacteria. Time to pucker up.

Palak Paneer

This vegetarian Indian dish typically features cubes of soft, mild paneer cheese floating in a bright-green spinach puree. It's on almost every Indian restaurant menu, but you can make it at home with a few special ingredients, like garam masala.

SERVES 4

RED PEPPERS
4 red bell peppers

1 cup water

½ cup apple cider vinegar

⅓ cup sugar

¼ cup kosher salt

PALAK PANEER
1 pound spinach, chopped

2 tablespoons Cultured Kefir Butter (page 35)

1 medium yellow onion, sliced

1 tablespoon minced fresh ginger

1 tablespoon garam masala

1 cinnamon stick

1 teaspoon ground cardamom

1 teaspoon smoked paprika

2 cloves garlic, sliced

1 large tomato, diced

2 tablespoons Kefir Labneh (page 43)

¼ cup organic plain whole-milk kefir

1 tablespoon kosher salt

Juice of ½ lemon

FOR SERVING
1½ cups Kefir Farmer Cheese (page 48), crumbled

Naan bread

FOR THE RED PEPPERS Place the peppers in a 500°F oven until the skin starts to char, 10 to 12 minutes. Remove the peppers from the oven, place in a bowl, and cover with a lid or plastic wrap. Set aside for 30 minutes, or until the peppers are cool enough to handle. Remove the stem from each pepper and cut them in half. Remove the skins and seeds and rinse. Discard the stems, skins, and seeds. Julienne cut the peppers and set aside in a bowl.

In a saucepot, boil the water, vinegar, sugar, and salt over high heat for 3 minutes. Pour this mixture over the peppers and steep overnight.

FOR THE PALAK PANEER In a saucepan, bring about 3 tablespoons water to a boil over medium-high heat and add the chopped spinach. Sauté for 1 minute or until tender. Drain and set aside. Melt the kefir butter in the same pan over medium-high heat. Add the onion, ginger, garam masala, cinnamon stick, cardamom, and paprika and sauté until translucent, about 5 minutes. Add the garlic and tomato and simmer for 15 minutes, then slowly stir in the labneh, then the kefir. Add the salt and lemon juice and simmer for 30 minutes.

Remove the cinnamon from the pan and add the chopped spinach. Simmer for 1 minute.

TO PLATE Divide the mixture among four bowls, topping with the red peppers and farmer cheese. Serve with warm naan.

Grilled Lamb Chops with Kefir Verde Sauce

Step up your marinade game by soaking lamb chops in tart pomegranate juice and tenderizing kefir. The chops will develop a beautiful caramelization during grilling, thanks to the natural sugars in the marinade.

SERVES 4

LAMB

1 teaspoon freshly cracked black pepper

2 tablespoons Maldon sea salt

3 cloves garlic, minced

1¼ cups organic plain whole-milk kefir

½ cup chopped fresh mint

1½ cups fresh or bottled pomegranate juice

8 lamb chops

VERDE SAUCE

2 bunches green onions, whole

2 tablespoons extra virgin olive oil

½ tablespoon Maldon sea salt

1 clove garlic, peeled

1 cup fresh chopped parsley

1 cup organic plain whole-milk kefir

FOR THE LAMB In a bowl that is large enough to accommodate the lamb, combine the black pepper, sea salt, garlic, kefir, mint, and pomegranate juice. Add the lamb, stirring well to coat, and let it marinate in the refrigerator overnight. Take the lamb out of the refrigerator 1 hour before cooking (discard the marinade).

Fire up your outdoor grill to very hot. Wipe the grill grates with a bit of oil and grill the lamb on high, about 5 minutes per side. Set the chops aside and let them rest for 10 minutes. (If you don't have an outdoor grill, you can use a grill pan or cast-iron skillet.)

FOR THE VERDE SAUCE In a medium bowl, toss the green onions with the olive oil and sea salt and cook on the grill until blackened. Set aside to cool. In a blender, combine the blackened green onions, garlic, parsley, and kefir and puree until smooth.

TO PLATE Serve the lamb family-style on a large platter, with the verde on the side.

DESSERTS

End your meals on a high note with any of these irresistible finishing touches, which include an updated take on red velvet cake, a world-class chocolatier's white chocolate kefir chia pudding, and an ethereally smooth panna cotta that will haunt your dreams.

Probiotics love cold temperatures—kefir cultures can live in the freezer for up to three years without losing their probiotic potential—so the Piccolo Bambino Chocolate Gelato (page 294), Lemongrass Kefir Ice Cream (page 292), and Roman Nutella Kefir Banana Pops (page 274) are an ideal way to get some sweet bacteria into your belly.

As for the desserts that require you to bake with kefir or kefir butter, get ready to dive into supermoist, tender cakes and flaky pie crust, all with more nutrients than their kefir-free counterparts.

Nothing here is crazily over-the-top sweet, yet every treat explodes with flavor, and is totally crave-worthy.

Roman Nutella Kefir Banana Pops

Creamy frozen banana kefir bathed in melted dark chocolate and dunked in hazelnut crumbles. I like to freeze a big batch of these four-ingredient pops in anticipation of a hot summer day. Kids love them because they're covered in chocolate; adults love them because they're like a grown-up, better-for-you version of those frozen chocolate-dipped bananas on a stick from their youth. I use hazelnuts, because they taste great with dark chocolate, provide a bit of protein, and remind me of the Nutella my mom used to import, but coconut flakes, goji berries, pumpkin seeds, or dehydrated strawberry bits would work well, too. (Or skip the nuts altogether if you have a nut-free household.)

SERVES 4

2 bananas, peeled

1 cup organic plain whole-milk kefir

1 cup dark chocolate chips, melted

½ cup hazelnuts, crushed

In a blender, puree the bananas and kefir together. Pour the blended mixture into your favorite pop mold and freeze overnight.

In a heat-proof bowl set over a pan of simmer water, melt the chocolate, stirring constantly. Once the chocolate has melted, remove it from the heat and, working quickly, remove the pops from the freezer. Pop them out of the molds and roll them in the melted chocolate, then lay them on waxed paper and return to the freezer for 5 minutes to set briefly. Remove them once again and roll them in the crushed hazelnuts, pressing gently to help them adhere. Freeze until serving.

PROBIOTIC POWER

Probiotics survive the freezing process, so these pops are alive with both flavor and health. (The same goes for the Frozen Kefir Pops with Lucky Fruit, page 296.)

Vanilla Crema Catalana

When I first began running, U2 was at the top of my playlist. So many of my runs took place against the backdrop of "Beautiful Day," "Where the Streets Have No Name," and "I Still Haven't Found What I'm Looking For."

In 2003, I bought two tickets to see U2 live in Barcelona with a friend. The only person who was worthy of that second golden ticket was my mom. And so it came to be that my then-sixty-year-old mama wound up flying to Spain with me for the most incredible outdoor U2 concert, the kind where the stadium shakes with energy, and, when Bono purposefully goes silent, thousands of people sing the entire chorus for him.

After the concert, the area outside the stadium was pure madness, teeming with fans and not a taxi to be seen. (This was during the pre-Uber era.) My mother and I walked for miles back toward our hotel, reminiscing about the concert and just chatting about life in general. Sometime after midnight, we stopped for dessert: vanilla crema catalana.* This recipe is in honor of that special, music-infused vacation and all the memories we made while in Barcelona.

SERVES 6

2 cups organic plain whole-milk kefir

Zest of ½ orange

Zest of ½ lemon

1 teaspoon vanilla extract

1 cinnamon stick

7 large egg yolks

½ cup plus 6 tablespoons sugar

1 heaping teaspoon cornstarch

Candied orange peel, for garnish

With my mom at the U2 concert in Barcelona.

* *Crema catalana is a Spanish take on the classic French dessert, crème brûlée.*

In a saucepan, combine the kefir, orange zest, lemon zest, vanilla, and cinnamon gently bring the mixture to a boil over medium heat. Remove the pan from the heat and allow the flavors to infuse for 15 minutes.

Meanwhile, in a bowl, whisk the egg yolks, ½ cup of the sugar, and the cornstarch together until pale and creamy.

Strain the infused kefir mixture through a fine-mesh sieve set over a bowl. Return the kefir to the pan and set over medium heat. Just before it begins to boil, slowly add the egg mixture, whisking constantly until it begins to thicken and coats the back of a wooden spoon, about 7 minutes. Remove the pan from the heat and pour the mixture into six individual dishes or ramekins. Cover each *crema* serving with a round of waxed paper to prevent a skin from forming and let them cool before placing them in the refrigerator. Refrigerate them for at least 1 hour.

Remove the waxed paper, sprinkle 1 tablespoon of sugar on top of each *crema* and caramelize using a blowtorch. (Alternatively, you can place the sugared *cremas* on a baking sheet under the broiler for a few minutes, until the sugar turns dark brown.) Allow the sugar to harden, then serve immediately, topped with candied orange peel.

Not So Red Velvet Cake

With its brilliant scarlet hue and contrasting bright white cream cheese frosting, red velvet cake is a real stunner. It's also loaded with artificial food coloring. I try to avoid cooking with food coloring, so this cake calls for red beet powder. Here's the thing about red beet powder, though: When you heat it in the oven, it turns brown. So I'm re-christening this recipe the Not So Red Velvet Cake. It still has the same subtle cocoa flavor, but without the fake dyes.

I like to tear the baked cake apart and layer it with the kefir buttercream, almost like a trifle. My kids always manage to stick their hands into any cake I bake—cake tastes better when you eat it off your fingers, right?—so I gave up my attempt at presentation perfection and decided to go the deconstruction route.

SERVES 8

CAKE

¾ cup (1½ sticks/6 ounces) Cultured Kefir Butter (page 35) or coconut oil

2¼ cups whole wheat flour, plus more for dusting

1½ teaspoons baking soda

Pinch of kosher salt

2 large brown eggs

1 cup organic plain whole-milk kefir

1 tablespoon distilled white vinegar

1 teaspoon vanilla extract

2 tablespoons unsweetened cocoa powder, plus more for garnish

2 tablespoons beet powder (I like ColorKitchen)

1½ cups coconut sugar

BUTTERCREAM

1 cup (2 sticks/8 ounces) Cultured Kefir Butter (page 35)

2 cups coconut sugar

1 teaspoon vanilla extract

2 cups Kefir Labneh (page 43)

FOR THE CAKE Preheat the oven to 350°F. Use some of the kefir butter to grease two 9-inch cake pans, then dust them with a little flour.

In a small bowl, combine the flour, baking soda, and salt. In another small bowl, beat the eggs, kefir, vinegar, and vanilla together until fully incorporated. In a third small bowl, mix the cocoa powder, beet powder, and enough warm water to make a paste. In a mixer, beat the kefir butter and coconut sugar until the mixture is light and fluffy, scraping down the sides of the bowl. While mixing slowly, add one-third of the flour mixture; mix until incorporated, about 30 seconds. To this mixture, add half of the kefir mixture, mixing until smooth. Add another one-third of the flour mixture and mix, then beat in the remaining kefir mixture. Add the final one-third of the flour mixture and mix until smooth. Lastly, add the cocoa/beet paste and mix until consistent in color.

Pour the batter mixture into the two greased pans and bake until a knife inserted in the center comes out clean, 25 to 30 minutes. Set aside to cool.

FOR THE BUTTERCREAM In a mixer, beat the kefir butter, coconut sugar, and vanilla until fluffy. Add the labneh in small amounts, whipping until fully incorporated. Refrigerate

TO PLATE Spread some of the buttercream on a platter. Use your hands to tear the cooled cake into uneven pieces, about the size of a tennis ball; arrange them atop the buttercream. With a spatula, spread a bit of buttercream on each piece of cake. Dust with cocoa powder and serve.

STEP-SAVER Use store-bought grass-fed butter to save time.

CHEF'S TIPS

Don't be afraid to try this buttercream on other types of cakes; yellow, chocolate, carrot. It's also delicious on its own with fresh berries.

When greasing pans with stick butter, keep your hands clean with this trick: Partially unwrap a stick of butter and hold it by the wrapped end as you use it to rub butter over the pan's surface.

Hibiscus Strawberry Rhubarb Pie

For years, my mom imported hibiscus tea from Germany—truckloads of it, in fact. Her warehouse was stacked from floor to ceiling with cases of it neatly arranged like a giant Tetris game come to life, and its aromatic fragrance permeated the air for what seemed like an entire block. To this day, I love brewing a cup of it and drinking it hot in the winter, iced in the summer. The tart, almost cranberry-esque flavor and deep magenta color lure me in every time. Don't forget to stop and appreciate the smell of the hibiscus as it steeps.

Hibiscus and rhubarb are a classic summertime combination; sweet, seasonal strawberries help balance all that terrific tartness. You'll be making this crimson treat over and over.

SERVES 6 TO 8

FILLING

4 cups finely diced rhubarb (make sure to select rhubarb that is deep red in color)

1 pound strawberries, trimmed and finely diced (about 4 cups)

2 tablespoons dried hibiscus flower petals

¼ cup honey

2 cups water

Generous pinch of kosher salt

1 tablespoon sherry vinegar

½ cup chopped fresh mint

½ cup chopped fresh basil

PIE CRUST

1 cup whole wheat flour, sifted

1 teaspoon kosher salt

1 cup (8 ounces) Cultured Kefir Butter (page 35), chilled and cubed

½ cup ice water

TOPPING

1 cup heavy whipping cream (32–36% butterfat)

2 tablespoons sugar

1 teaspoon vanilla extract

¼ cup organic plain whole-milk kefir

FOR THE FILLING In a deep heat-proof bowl, mix the rhubarb and strawberries.

In a large saucepan, combine the hibiscus, honey, water, and kosher salt and bring the mixture to a boil over medium-high heat. Boil for 2 to 3 minutes, then pour it over the strawberries and rhubarb. Allow to fruit to steep until cool.

Once cooled, drain the strawberries and rhubarb in a sieve set over a bowl to catch the liquid. Return the fruit to its original bowl. Transfer the steeping liquid to a saucepan, bring to a simmer, and cook to reduce to a syrup, 8 to 10 minutes. Allow the syrup to cool. Once it has cooled, fold it back into the strawberries and rhubarb, then add the sherry vinegar, mint, and basil. Mix and let stand.

FOR THE PIE CRUST Preheat the oven to 425°F.

In a bowl, combine the flour and salt. Using a pastry cutter, cut the butter into the flour until it is incorporated and sandy. Slowly add the ice water to the bowl and mix quickly until the dough is just barely incorporated, then let the dough rest in the refrigerator for 30 minutes.

Turn the dough out onto a floured, chilled work surface. Using the palm of your hand, push out from the center of the dough until the dough smears across the surface. Scrape this back to the center of the mound and rotate the dough 90 degrees, repeating the process until the dough has turned three times. Form the dough into a ball, cover it with plastic wrap, and return it to the refrigerator for another 30 minutes

Unwrap the dough and let it rest for 5 minutes at room temperature. Using a rolling pin, hit the middle of the ball of dough once, then turn it 90 degrees and hit it again; you will see a cross in the middle of the dough. Now, begin to roll out the dough, turning it 90 degrees each time until it is about ¼ inch thick. Fold the dough in half, and in half again. Place the corner of the folded dough in the center of a standard 9-inch pie pan and unfold, working the dough into the shape of the pan. Let this rest in the refrigerator for 15 minutes, uncovered.

Place a piece of parchment paper into the pie shell and fill it with pie weights, uncooked rice, or dried beans. Place the pie shell in the center of the oven and bake for about 15 minutes. Remove the parchment and weights and return to the oven and bake for another 5 to 7 minutes until the crust is golden brown. Let it cool on a rack.

FOR THE TOPPING In the chilled bowl of a mixer, combine the heavy cream, sugar, and vanilla and beat until stiff peaks form. Gently fold in the kefir.

TO PLATE Fill the pie shell with the fruit and syrup mixture, then top it with the whipped cream mixture.

STEP-SAVER Use store-bought pie crust to save time. Or skip the crust altogether and enjoy the filling and topping on their own.

DID YOU KNOW . . .

Hibiscus tea has been shown to lower blood pressure; in some studies, it works as well as certain blood pressure medications.

Lemon Icebox Pie in a Jar

Before I knew I was pregnant with Misha, I had the most intense cravings for lemon curd. The kind of cravings where I would throw daggers at you if you didn't give me what I wanted . . . and lemon curd isn't exactly the easiest thing to find. One morning I woke in a hotel room in Mexico over the holidays, and all I could think about was lemon curd. I called room service for help with my emergency lemon curd needs and they had no clue what I was talking about. The chef got on the phone and said he was not familiar with the recipe. So I explained to him, as quickly as I could, how to make it. And I got my fix.

To this day, Misha loves lemon anything. Every time I make this pie, she retells to me the story of how when she was in my belly, she made me eat lemon curd every chance she could. Like a boss.

SERVES 4

EGG YOLK MIXTURE/MERINGUE

4 large brown eggs, separated

1 cup granulated sugar

Juice of 2 lemons

¼ cup Kefir Labneh (page 43)

WHIPPED CREAM

¼ cup heavy whipping cream (32–36% butterfat)

2 tablespoons powdered sugar

FOR SERVING

1 prebaked pie crust, store-bought or the crust from Hibiscus Strawberry Rhubarb Pie (page 283)

4 canning jars

FOR THE EGG YOLK MIXTURE In a mixer, whip the egg yolks with ½ cup of the granulated sugar until thick. Stir in the lemon juice and transfer the mixture to a glass bowl. Set the bowl over a pan of simmering water and cook, constantly stirring, until it thickens, 6 to 8 minutes. Remove it from the heat and allow it to cool. Once the egg yolk mixture is cool, fold in the labneh.

FOR THE MERINGUE Clean out the original mixer bowl, then beat the egg whites and the remaining ½ cup granulated sugar, whipping until soft peaks form. Fold the meringue into the cooled egg yolk mixture.

FOR THE WHIPPED CREAM In a bowl, with a hand mixer, beat the heavy cream with the powdered sugar until soft peaks form.

TO PLATE Crumble the pie crust and pour a small amount into the bottom of each of the canning jars. Divide the lemon mousse among the four jars, topping each with an equal amount of whipped cream. Cover each jar with a lid and freeze before serving.

CHEF'S TIP This sweet-and-tart, no-bake pie recipe has the luxurious texture of key lime pie, and the jars make them picnic-ready.

Raspberry Bread Pudding

This dessert is the perfect chance to breathe new life into day-old bread, which actually works even better than fresh; the drier the bread, the more creamy goodness it will soak up. I like sourdough, because it gives the dish some body and bakes up a little crispy around the edges, but you can also use brioche, challah, or French baguettes. Serve it for dessert, yes, but it also reigns supreme at brunch.

SERVES 4

1 cup heavy whipping cream (32–36% butterfat)

¼ cup Kefir Labneh (page 43)

1 cup organic plain whole-milk kefir

4 large brown eggs

1 cup sugar

1 loaf sourdough bread, chopped into 1-inch cubes

2 cups raspberries

Butter, for greasing

Preheat the oven to 375°F.

In a small saucepan, stir together the cream, labneh, and kefir. Bring to a boil over medium-high heat. Meanwhile, in a mixer, whip the eggs with the sugar. Once the kefir/cream is boiling, whisk a bit of the hot mixture into the egg mixture to temper them. Then slowly add the tempered egg mixture to the hot kefir/cream and slowly incorporate the two, cooking until thick but not boiling.

PROBIOTIC POWER

Sourdough is a fermented food. Bacteria and yeast in the dough boost its acidity, infusing it with its characteristic tangy taste.

Place the bread cubes in a bowl and pour the hot kefir-cream-egg all over them. Let sit for 20 minutes. Fold in all but a few of the raspberries.

Grease a 9-inch deep baking dish and fill it with the bread mixture, packing the cubes in side by side. Bake the pudding for 30 minutes. Once the pudding is cool to the touch, scoop it out into four bowls and garnish with the remaining raspberries.

Lemongrass Kefir Ice Cream

Don't be surprised if this bright, citrus-y ice cream leaves you feeling healthier; lemongrass is used medicinally in a variety of ways, from easing coughs and congestion in Ayurveda to reducing anxiety among the Brazilians to soothing sore muscles in Thai massage therapy. Studies have confirmed that lemongrass has antibacterial, antimicrobial power; in one study, lemongrass oil was found to be effective against a variety of unhealthy bacteria—the same ones that kefir's probiotics help to keep in check.

This ice cream's bright, clean flavor works well as a palate cleanser—similar to lemon sorbet—or as a sweet finale to your meal.

SERVES 4

2 lemongrass stalks

3 cups heavy whipping cream (32–36% butterfat)

6 large egg yolks

1 cup sugar

3 cups organic plain whole-milk kefir

Fresh berries, for garnish

Cut the lemongrass in half lengthwise and pound it with the back of a knife to release its oils. In a saucepan, combine the lemongrass and cream and bring to a boil over medium-high heat. Meanwhile, in a mixer, whip the eggs yolks with the sugar until frothy.

Slowly whisk a small amount of the hot cream into the egg mixture to temper it. Then whisk in the remaining cream mixture, adding it in a slow, steady stream. Whisk everything together, then return it to the saucepan and cook until it thickens, but don't allow it to boil. Refrigerate the custard mixture until cool, then strain the lemongrass out of it and discard.

Combine the custard with the kefir and transfer to an ice cream machine. Churn until thick and creamy. When serving, garnish with fresh berries for a pretty pop of color.

Piccolo Bambino
Chocolate Gelato

Lemongrass Kefir
Ice Cream

Piccolo Bambino Chocolate Gelato

When my parents and I were in immigration limbo—out of the Soviet Union but not yet in the United States—we called Italy our home for three months. The people we encountered while in Rome were friendly and welcoming toward us; my mom used to tell me how the gelato shop owners, recognizing that my parents could not afford their icy treats, would offer me free cones, calling me, piccolo bambino (little child). This kefir- and cream-based gelato doubles down on the chocolate, thanks to melted dark chocolate as well as cocoa powder.

SERVES 4

4 ounces dark chocolate (85% cacao), coarsely chopped

3 cups heavy whipping cream (32–36% butterfat)

6 large egg yolks

1 cup sugar

¼ cup unsweetened cocoa powder

3 cups organic plain whole-milk kefir

SUGGESTED TOPPINGS (2 TABLESPOONS EACH)

Banana slices

Chocolate chunks

Hazelnuts

In a medium heat-proof bowl set over a pan of simmering water, melt the chocolate, stirring constantly. Set aside.

In a saucepan, bring the cream to a boil over medium-high heat. While the cream is warming up, in a mixer, whip the eggs yolks with the sugar until frothy. Slowly whisk a small amount of the hot cream into the egg mixture to temper it. Then whisk in the remaining cream mixture, adding it in a slow, steady stream. Whisk everything together, then return it to the saucepan and cook until it thickens, but don't allow it to boil.

Once the mixture has the texture of a thin custard (just thick enough to lightly coat a spoon), slowly add a small amount of it to the melted chocolate and whisk until fully incorporated, then add in the remainder of the cream mixture and whisk again. Once all of the cream has been incorporated, whisk in the cocoa powder, then the kefir. Chill in the refrigerator. Transfer the cooled mixture to an ice cream machine and churn until thick and creamy.

My parents couldn't afford gelato when we were exiled in Rome. I'm always humbled when Misha and Leah have the opportunity to enjoy some, especially in Italy.

Frozen Kefir Pops with Lucky Fruit

The tradition of eating twelve grapes in twelve seconds on New Year's Eve originated in Spain; revelers hold twelve grapes in their hands and wait for Madrid's Puerta del Sol clock tower to begin ringing out the final twelve seconds of the year. With the first chime, Spaniards pop a grape into their mouth. A second grape accompanies the second chime, then a third, and a fourth . . . if all twelve have been consumed by midnight then, legend says, you are guaranteed good luck in el año nuevo.

The lucky grapes tradition has since been adopted by several Latin American countries. Our family usually spends New Year's Eve in Mexico, where our hotel ensures we get to partake in the twelve grapes tradition. They leave little cellophane baggies on our beds, each containing a dozen grapes. We all sit down together and set our intentions for the New Year, each of us naming twelve wishes aloud—one wish for each month of the coming year. I remind our girls that they hold the power to make their dreams come true.

This frozen treat was inspired by the twelve grapes tradition. It's hard to fit a dozen grapes into a pop mold, though, so cut them in half and add just a few; it's the thought that counts. This recipe also works well with other fruit, like peaches, pitted cherries, and berries.

SERVES 8

3½ cups organic plain whole-milk kefir

2 tablespoons honey

1 cup seedless grapes, halved (or your favorite fruit, chopped)

In a bowl, mix the kefir with the honey. Divide the fruit among eight 4-ounce pop molds, then top them with honeyed kefir, filling each mold all the way up. Freeze until set or overnight.

Green Tea Cheesecake

The moment Leah said, "Pandas come from China and eat bamboo" when she was two years old, I knew I wanted to take her on an adventure to that part of the world. Six years later, we were in China. We climbed the Great Wall, visited Tiananmen Square and Hong Kong's Big Buddha, and rode sidecars in Shanghai. We ate dim sum, mochi ice cream, sampled every variety of dumpling you could imagine—including some shaped like Hello Kitty—and came "thisclose" to trying fried scorpions. We also met a Chinese tea master, who showed us how to dry green tea leaves and use them to make tea, which we then enjoyed in a traditional ceremony.

When we returned home with all the tea in China, I was trying to figure out a way to marry its grassy, earthy flavor with a dish that represents home for me. Chicago is known for a handful of things; the biting wind off of Lake Michigan, deep-dish pizza, mobsters, and cheesecake. Cheesecake is such a perfect blank canvas for color and flavor, so I thought, "Why not combine the green tea we brought home with cheesecake?" That's how this recipe came to be. It's my take on buttermilk ricotta cheesecake, using creamy farmer cheese instead.

CRUST

13 graham cracker rectangles, crushed

6 tablespoons coconut oil, melted

2 tablespoons coconut sugar

FILLING

4 tablespoons matcha green tea powder

3/4 cup warm water

4 cups Kefir Farmer Cheese (page 48)

2/3 cup organic plain whole-milk kefir

1 cup powdered sugar

2 teaspoons vanilla extract

Fresh raspberries, for garnish

PROBIOTIC POWER

My dad would have loved this cheesecake; when he and my mom started manufacturing farmer cheese in the '80s, the process left them with tons of excess product. Rather than let it go to waste, they used it to create and sell America its first farmer cheese-based cheesecake.

DID YOU KNOW . . .

There are 54 grams of protein in this entire cheesecake, thanks to the farmer cheese—about twice as much as a typical commercially prepared cheesecake.

FOR THE CRUST In a bowl, combine the crushed graham crackers, melted coconut oil, and coconut sugar, mixing with your hands until crumbly. Press the mixture into the bottom of a standard 9-inch springform pan until it is evenly distributed.

FOR THE FILLING In a small bowl, mix together the matcha and water to form a paste. In a bowl, with a hand mixer, beat together the farmer cheese, kefir, powdered sugar, and vanilla. Beat in the matcha paste until it is well incorporated.

TO ASSEMBLE Pour the mixture over the crust in the springform. Place the pie in the refrigerator on top of a large plate or folded towel, as the farmer cheese will release a good amount of water and whey as it sets.

Refrigerate the cheesecake for at least 3 hours or, preferably, overnight. Garnish with fresh raspberries.

NOTE For individual desserts, you can halve this recipe and use small jam jars instead of a springform pan.

STEP-SAVER Use store-bought farmer cheese and pie crust to save time.

Mary's Panna Cotta with Red Wine Syrup

Music and food make the world a better, more colorful, more delicious place. When Pearl Jam released their first album, Ten, I was an ambitious, flannel-wearing, espresso-drinking high school junior, full of raw teenage emotion, confusion, and angst. Eddie Vedder's lyrics of fierce honesty and social commentary validated all that I was feeling and thinking. Pearl Jam's music became both a mirror and a coming-of-age soundtrack.

I've since seen them in concert more than forty-five times, and I always leave feeling intoxicated with passion, analyzing the set list and replaying my favorite parts in my head. The excitement I feel before a show today is the same I felt as a teenager; the only thing that's changed is my seats have gotten better. At the breathtakingly spiritual Gorge Amphitheatre near Seattle, it was 106 degrees outside and I was all alone. I had just ended a long relationship, and I experienced a sense of freedom, independence, and renewal as "Black" reverberated off the walls of the massive slices of sandstone surrounding us, the sky an ombré of brick red, marigold, and saffron. At Madison Square Garden, I was eight months pregnant with Leah and felt her rocking out inside by belly right along with me. At the Ziggo Dome in Amsterdam, Jason was by my side; earlier that morning, I had gotten into a terrible bicycle accident—bad enough that I was taken by ambulance to the emergency room—but I still insisted on seeing Eddie perform, hobbling to the concert, loaded up on pain medicine and determination.

Eddie starts every show by walking onstage with a bottle of red wine and a notebook. During one such concert, he passed his bottle of red into the front row as he sang the chorus of "Crazy Mary," encouraging the crowd to drink up and pass the bottle down. The glossy, rich red wine sauce spooned over a silken panna cotta, reminds me of that night. The alcohol cooks out of the sauce, so be sure to pour yourself a glass of your favorite red with it. Then be sure to pass it around.

PROBIOTIC POWER

Wine-drinkers have a more diverse—and therefore healthier—array of gut bacteria than nondrinkers.

PANNA COTTA

3½ sheets gelatin

2 cups heavy whipping cream (32–36% butterfat)

1 cup sugar

2 cups organic plain whole-milk kefir

½ cup Kefir Labneh (page 43)

RED WINE SYRUP

One 750 ml bottle red wine (your choice)

½ cup honey

1 teaspoon freshly cracked black pepper

FOR SERVING

Sliced peaches and pomegranate seeds (arils), for garnish

FOR THE PANNA COTTA Submerge the gelatin in an ice bath for 10 minutes, then drain well. In a small saucepan, bring the cream to a light simmer over medium heat. Add the drained gelatin to the pan with the cream (still over heat) and whisk in the sugar. Cook for 2 minutes until the sugar is fully dissolved.

In a bowl, combine the kefir and labneh, then add the warm cream mixture to the bowl and combine until fully incorporated. Pour this mixture into eight 6-ounce ramekins or custard molds. Allow it to set in the refrigerator overnight.

FOR THE RED WINE SYRUP Pour the bottle of wine into a small, heavy-bottomed pot and add the honey and black pepper. Cook the wine until all the alcohol is gone and it is reduced to a thick syrup (about ½ cup). Pour the syrup through a fine-mesh sieve into a bowl to remove the pepper. Refrigerate the syrup until you are ready to garnish the panna cotta.

TO PLATE Remove the panna cotta from the refrigerator 15 minutes before serving. Fill a bowl with hot tap water and dip each panna cotta mold into the water, then turn out onto individual plates. Garnish with sliced peaches and pomegranate seeds (arils) and drizzle with the red wine syrup.

Apricot Coconut White Chocolate Pudding

RECIPE COURTESY OF KATRINA MARKOFF

This gorgeous dessert comes from Katrina Markoff of Vosges (the same friend who helped me with the Cricket Smoothie, page 114). I first learned of Katrina in a business magazine more than a decade ago, when I read about her being named Bon Appétit's Food Artisan of the Year and stalked her until she agreed to meet me for dinner. We instantly became close friends, mentors to one another, and partners in fearlessness. Katrina not only taught me how to eat a piece of chocolate guilt-free, but how to turn it into a sensual experience that touches all parts of the body.

Here's how Katrina describes the creative process behind this dessert:

I enjoy making healthy desserts and snacks for myself as well as my kids. This dessert concept feels indulgent but light at the same time. The sourness of the kefir plays really well with the white chocolate and it comes out almost like a white ganache, but not as sweet; it's just sweet enough. Because the cold kefir isn't folded in until the end, it retains its probiotic powers.

SERVES 4

PUDDING

1 cup plus 2 tablespoons chopped white chocolate

3½ cups organic plain whole-milk kefir

¼ cup chia seeds

¾ cup toasted coconut flakes, plus more for garnish

⅓ cup chopped dried apricots, plus more for garnish

CANDIED PECANS

¼ cup coconut sugar

2 teaspoons water

1 cup pecans

FOR SERVING

8 slices red plum

Handful edible flowers

FOR THE PUDDING In a heat-proof medium bowl set over a pan of gently simmering water, melt the white chocolate, stirring. Once melted, slowly stir in the kefir, then the chia seeds, coconut flakes, and chopped apricots. Scrape the chocolate/kefir mixture into four small glasses, cover, and refrigerate for at least 20 minutes.

FOR THE CANDIED PECANS In a saucepan, combine the coconut sugar and water and melt over low heat. Meanwhile, place the pecans in a microwave-safe dish and microwave for 20 to 30 seconds. Once the sugar is completely melted and the mixture begins to simmer, add the pecans and remove the pan from the heat. Stir the pecans constantly, until the mixture dries and the pecans are evenly coated. Spread the pecans out on a dish and allow them to cool.

TO PLATE Garnish each glass with sliced red plums, dried apricots, candied pecans, edible flowers, and more toasted coconut flakes.

TIP You can find edible flowers at many grocery stores; look near the fresh herbs section. Or, grow your own. Marigolds, pansies, nasturtium, orchids, and roses are all edible. Just make sure not to spray them with pesticides.

Do you know a young woman in high school or college who dreams of working in the food industry? Vosges's sister company, Wild Ophelia, has an Accelerator Program that provides ambitious girls with the funds and mentorship necessary to start a business. Budding foodie #GirlBosses can apply at www.wildophelia.com.

Sweet Potato Pie

A few years ago, Jason and I were in a cab during a family Thanksgiving trip to Phoenix and Scottsdale, when our driver started talking about how excited he was for Thanksgiving dinner. Out of nowhere, Jason asked the driver (his name was Anthony, I remember like it was yesterday) if his grandmother would be baking sweet potato pie. Anthony said yes, she was, and Jason then asked, "Can she save me a slice?" It was so unlike J—he tends to be on the quieter side—that I burst out laughing. Then I decided that I would bake him his very own pie, so he wouldn't have to beg random cabdrivers.

Nutmeg, cinnamon, and cloves are the magical trifecta of holiday baking. Here, they come together in the form of a picture-perfect Thanksgiving classic, sweet potato pie.

SERVES 4

3 medium sweet potatoes, unpeeled

2 large brown eggs

½ cup honey

1 cup organic plain whole-milk kefir

Zest of 1 lemon

⅛ teaspoon freshly grated nutmeg

⅛ teaspoon ground cloves

⅛ teaspoon ground cinnamon

Pinch of kosher salt

1 unbaked store-bought pie shell

½ cup Kefir Labneh (page 43)

Pecans, for garnish

Preheat the oven to 375°F.

Stab the potatoes a few times with a paring knife. Place the potatoes on a baking sheet and roast until fully tender, about 1 hour. Once the potatoes are cool enough to handle, scoop out the insides and place the flesh in a large bowl and mash them with a fork. Add the eggs, honey, kefir, lemon zest, nutmeg, cloves, cinnamon, and salt and mix well. Pour the mixture into the pie shell and bake until just set, about 45 minutes. Allow the pie to cool before enjoying. Serve topped with labneh and pecans.

ACKNOWLEDGMENTS

I wrote an effing book. I've been wanting to write a book since I was a fourteen-year-old kid in creative writing class, searching for words and stories worthy of print. I don't think I actually planned on writing a cookbook, but as I reflect, it's obvious that telling parts of my family's story through recipes and food would be the perfect medium. Now I will try to thank everyone who has helped me in this process. There are too many people to list, but you know who you are and I am eternally grateful for the role you've played in my and my family's life . . . big or small . . . there are no coincidences and there are no chance encounters. We can call it the butterfly effect.

Leslie Goldman. Lolly. Friend. Trusted confidant. Work wife. Fact checker. Project manager. From the minute I got naked with you (literally, we were naked when we met in our gym's locker room) you have been encouraging me to find my voice, helping me find my words, editing me, and holding

my hand when panic strikes. From introducing me to Laura Nolan (now *our* agent) to taking the words that mostly existed in my head and transforming them into words in beautiful black and white, neatly organized on pages ready to be turned, there is no way this book would have been written without you. Period. I am eternally grateful (and I love you more than any words or unnecessary parentheses can express).

Jeffery Zurofsky. JZ. Kitchen wizard. Work husband. It's hard to call it work when it's so much fun and such a joy. While I have spent most of my entire life in the food business, I am not a trained culinary chef. We met on that beach in Tulum and you stole the last bite of *tacos de hoja santa* and *cochinitha pelon Mexicano* right out of my mouth, then proceeded to slam down some much needed real talk in a matter of five minutes. I knew we would become good friends and that I wanted to work with you. Indeed, you have become my friend and ally. You hold space better than almost anyone I know and I am grateful that the universe brought you to my side. You are the secret sauce to almost every recipe in this book. Thank you.

We all want someone to believe in us. Sincere gratitude to my agent, Laura Nolan; my editor, Julia Pastore; and the entire publishing team at HarperOne. Thank you for believing in me, for pushing and gently encouraging me, for backing off and extending my deadline when my life and the world disrupted the completion of this manuscript, and for reminding me that indeed, I am not an idiot, forty-eight hours before my first draft was due.

Jennifer Davick, Jeffery Larsen, Lena Yaremenko, and the entire photography and food styling team—thank you for bringing it all to life in the most beautiful way. I practically cried when I saw my family recipes all dressed up and looking so fancy. It has been a pleasure to work with you. A big thank-you to Lauren Volo, Marina Velasquez, and the rest of the team who came through in the final hour on last-minute photography and final touches I could not live without.

To the incredible and hardworking people at Lifeway Foods, past, present, and future (special shout-out to Derek Miller) and the countless agencies, consultants, lawyers (Doug Hass, Rick Kessler, and Tim Lavendar, I see you. Insert gratitude emoji), the farmers, suppliers, vendors, everyone who has ever worked with our products and our company, the drivers who transport ingredients and finished bottles of magic ancient history, the retailers who stock them, our customers who share their stories of how kefir has improved their health and healed their bodies . . . thank you for your loyalty, partnerships, and for giving us purpose for the hard work. Without you all, there would be nothing. Appreciation also goes out to the restaurateurs of the world, some of whom inspired many of the recipes in this book, and the food industry as a whole, a community that has opened its door and inspired my family and me, nurtured us, challenged us, and loved us.

To my various friends and contributors, I am in your debt: Christy Turlington Burns and the team at Every Mother Counts; Seamus Mullen; Jason Hammel; Katrina Markoff; Ina Pinkney; my UNF family.

To the Litvinsky, Fleyshman, Sikar, Nikolenko, and Groisman families: Thank you for your lifelong loyalty and friendship. You've been my family's shoulder to lean on. We've mourned and celebrated together, traveled and work together, eaten Olivier salad and drunk vodka together . . . lots of vodka. You're more than friends; you're our extended family by choice. These are your stories, too. *Nostrovia!* Bella Groisman, in particular, you were a strong, feisty woman with a can-do attitude, and you made a wonderful partner for my mom in the deli business.

To the Alters, Semmelhacks, Markoffs, Kotches, Kamms, Trivaxes, and Wiczykes: You're my people. We share a lot of meals together, and I love you. To the Reznik family: When destiny brought us together, a new Brady Bunch was born. I've never seen as thoughtful and kind brothers as the ones who've joined us. Thank you for loving on my mom and children as fiercely as you do. *L'chaim.*

DeeDee Goldman and Nancy Simon, thank you for everything. To Angie Garnopolsky, thank you for your unconditional love and friendship. See you at the beach. Or under a tree eating French silk pie.

To the people and the community in Chicago: This book is, in part, a love letter to the City of Broad Shoulders, a city that welcomed and sheltered a young starving immigrant family and provided countless opportunities and memories. It also happens to have some of the greatest food in this corner of the universe. The Windy City is *the* greatest city and we've been proud to call it home for over forty years.

Mom, you already know that you are my greatest role model, but I will say it again and again. I am so proud of you, of everything you have done, of the adversity you have overcome, and I am so grateful for all the sacrifices you've made to create a better life. I

know it was not easy. The story of hardworking immigrants and strong, fearless women is not a new one, but it's never been told this way. Writing this book and sharing parts of our life and your recipes only brought me to the sobering realization that it is actually impossible to do this story justice. There are so many more things to say and to share. For now, I will just say I love you.

Papa, I miss you. I miss your voice. I miss your ingenuity. I miss almost everything about you. I wish you were here to meet your granddaughters. But mostly I just wish you were here with us to see all that has transpired since you moved on. Your broken heart has left a big, gaping hole in mine. As complex as it all was, I would never trade it for anything. Thank you for pushing me, for pushing education on me, for putting strong female role models in front of me every chance you got, for teaching me everything you could in the short time we had together, for being brave and courageous when the moment came to risk it all, to leave your homeland, and to start a company. You believed in the power of kefir before anyone else did in this country. When people laughed and cast their doubts on a poor man with a strong Russian accent you paid no attention; you charged ahead and you did the hard work. You were the GREATEST storyteller I have ever met. That's why we are here today. You sacrificed your own health to bring health to everyone else. And if a customer called late at night in need of kefir somewhere across the country, I have no doubt you would get in the car and personally deliver it to them. I hope that wherever you are, you are finally resting in peace.

Eddie. Ed. Edward. My brother. From the moment I learned Mom was pregnant, I have loved you more than you will ever know. When you were born, I so wanted you to be a sister. I even remember the day we picked you up from Edgewater hospital and the security guard kept me company as I dangled my feet on the couch. I proudly told him, "I have a baby sister." I even gave you alternate female names and told my teachers you were a girl. It is what it is. We are who we are. This book could have very easily been written by both of us; after all, most of these stories are ours together. Book number two perhaps? I'm beyond proud of you and I know our father would be too. I know when he died, you were nowhere ready to take on the enormous responsibility thrown on your shoulders at the ripe old age of twenty-three, but you did. Honestly, I'm not surprised. Where I dragged home all my textbooks and spent hours trying to get smart, it came naturally for you. As I've watched you grow from a baby to a boy to a man, all I can say is that I am proud of you and so grateful for you. I have so many fond memories of our childhood. Like jumping on a plane in the evening and being at the Eiffel Tower by morning while Dad drafted a plan to see every work of art in France—and I do mean *every work of art*—while Mom ran to the gourmet market for a fresh crispy baguette, smoked salmon, Brie, and foie gras for our traditional picnic in our small hotel room. Or when you and Dad narrowly escaped a Turkish prison over a miscommunication at the Grand Bazaar in Istanbul, concluding with the best gyros we have ever eaten. Literally. Family business is no easy picnic. It's challenging and it's painful and we struggle, but ultimately our love always gets us to where we need to be.

Jason, you anchor our family with strength, balance, and incredible patience. You've made heroic sacrifices so that I can go off and try to be a badass, all the while, redefining masculinity and challenging society. You've mastered both French braids and the art of living with three hardheaded, stubborn girls who know what they want and won't stop till they get it. You are honestly the greatest papa and life partner we could ever ask for. Our home and our life would not run seamlessly, or at all, without you. In the moments of greatest crisis and conflict, you are the family rabbi, handling every thorny situation with the steady hand that only a trained jeweler has. You are the keeper of secrets and passwords. We are all grateful that you stuck with our crazy clan; I'm shocked that my father's karaoke did not have you running out the door. This book and this life would not be possible without you. It just wouldn't. Thank you for being my best friend, supporting me, and being my partner in this journey and adventure. I love you. Through all time.

And lastly to my beautiful, smart, brave, and funny babies, Leah and Misha. You have been forced to taste-test every recipe I have ever made and there have certainly been a few fails. That horrific coffee cake I made with coconut flour? I'm sorry. You inspire me more than anyone. You make me want to live the fullest, most beautiful and joyful life, because more than anything, that's what I want for you. I have no doubt that you are well on your way to achieving all your dreams. I watch with fascination as you jump on YouTube, find a recipe and bravely start cooking up a storm in our kitchen, whether it's a cake, pancakes, or your own batch of fruit preserves using berries you picked at the farm. Oh, and so much pink slime and bubbling volcanic eruptions, too. Step by step, you meet every challenge that comes your way, just like your family and those who came before you. Your grandfather would have been very, very proud of you. I can see him now, beaming with pride. Never stop experimenting. Never stop being curious. Yes, you can be a singer, a dancer, a mommy, an artist, a chef, an astrophysicist, and the President. The stories in this book are your stories. They are your DNA. They tell of history and time before you were living beings, but they are undoubtedly yours. All my love through infinity and eternity, Mama.

INDEX